# SIMPLY THE GREATEST LIFE

*Finding Myself in the Country*

## DAVID SCHAFER

BALBOA.
PRESS

A DIVISION OF HAY HOUSE

Copyright © 2012 by David Schafer

All rights reserved. No part of this book may be used or reproduced by any means, graphic, electronic, or mechanical, including photocopying, recording, taping or by any information storage retrieval system without the written permission of the publisher except in the case of brief quotations embodied in critical articles and reviews.

ISBN: 978-1-4525-5845-5 (sc)
ISBN: 978-1-4525-5844-8 (e)
ISBN: 978-1-4525-5843-1 (hc)

Library of Congress Control Number: 2012916574

Balboa Press books may be ordered through booksellers or by contacting:

Balboa Press
A Division of Hay House
1663 Liberty Drive
Bloomington, IN 47403
www.balboapress.com
1-(877) 407-4847

Because of the dynamic nature of the Internet, any web addresses or links contained in this book may have changed since publication and may no longer be valid. The views expressed in this work are solely those of the author and do not necessarily reflect the views of the publisher, and the publisher hereby disclaims any responsibility for them.

The author of this book does not dispense medical advice or prescribe the use of any technique as a form of treatment for physical, emotional, or medical problems without the advice of a physician, either directly or indirectly. The intent of the author is only to offer information of a general nature to help you in your quest for emotional and spiritual well-being. In the event you use any of the information in this book for yourself, which is your constitutional right, the author and the publisher assume no responsibility for your actions.

Any people depicted in stock imagery provided by Thinkstock are models, and such images are being used for illustrative purposes only.

Certain stock imagery © Thinkstock.

Printed in the United States of America

Balboa Press rev. date: 11/07/12

# DEDICATION

This book is dedicated to Abe Kurtz, Amanda Riley, Ivan Schrock, Syl Graber, and Carl Miller of Jamesport, Ronnie Kincaid from Trenton and Bill Coon from Spickard, and especially Ernie Kauffman from Bloomfield, Iowa and Joel Salatin from Virginia.

Without these fine neighbors and friends the Featherman 'business from Heaven' would never have come about. And this book would have been the worse for it.

# Contents

Foreword..................................................................................IX

Introduction ....................................................................... XIII

Prologue ...............................................................................XV

**Part 1 – Green Homesteading**

Chapter 1 Bargaining for Paradise ..................................... 1

Chapter 2 The Ideal Location ........................................... 9

Chapter 3 Plan A: Timber Frame Home............................ 13

Chapter 4 From Giant Hogs to Three Little Pigs.................... 19

Chapter 5 A Home of Straw, Sticks … ............................... 27

Chapter 6 …and Stone .................................................... 35

Chapter 7 Horse Sense ................................................... 39

Chapter 8 On the Walls – Mud!........................................ 49

Chapter 9 Off the Walls: Henry Schrock's Cabinets.............. 59

Chapter 10 Off the Roof .................................................. 71

Chapter 11 Off the Grid................................................... 75

**Part 2 – Animal Companions**

Chapter 12 Good to Go.................................................... 81

Chapter 13 Lucky Years - Marketing ................................. 93

Chapter 14 More Lucky Years – Pet Sheep....................... 105

**Part 3 - Community**

Chapter 15 Market Day – A journal entry ........................ 117

Chapter 16 Community Development ............................... 123

Chapter 17 Pastured Poultry - Social Activism...................... 131

Chapter 18 Chicken Plucker Factory ......................................... 137

Chapter 19 James.......................................................................... 151

Chapter 20 My Amish Partner in Crime.................................... 157

**Part 4 – Tracking Myself**

Chapter 21 Tracker Influence ..................................................... 173

Chapter 22 Sweat Lodge .............................................................. 179

Chapter 23 Vision Quest .............................................................. 185

Chapter 24 Three Trackers........................................................... 191

Chapter 25 Finding Myself........................................................... 205

# FOREWORD

John Ikerd
**Professor Emeritus of Agricultural Economics**
**University of Missouri**

I FIRST MET DAVID Schafer sometime after I had returned to Missouri in the late 1980s. I had returned to the University of Missouri to provide leadership for a new sustainable agriculture program, after twenty years on the faculties of three other universities. Missouri was and is a major forage-producing state, and I thought grass-based livestock had tremendous potential for enhancing the sustainability of agriculture. David and Alice had been receiving some well-deserved positive publicity at the time for their grass-based beef cattle operation in North Missouri. They were founding members of the Green Hills Farm Project, a group of farmers in the North Central part of the state who are dedicated to growing livestock on grass, meaning without or with minimal feeding of grain.

On one occasion, talking with David, he suggested I "burn that report someone in your department just put out advocating concentrated animal feeding operations as a rural development strategy for Missouri." I told David I wasn't aware something of that nature had been published. He suggested instead an economic analysis that focused on the effect of local farmers spending money in their communities.

The report in question provided estimates of the numbers of jobs that would be created by typical large-scale confinement hog operations. My immediate question was: "How many people were already being employed producing the same number of hogs on independent family hog farms in Missouri?" My conclusion from a careful comparison was that three farmers or workers on independent hog farms would be displaced for every one job created by the new CAFO hog operations. Needless to say, my conclusions created quite a controversy in the College of Agriculture. I have been a reluctant combatant in the "CAFO wars" ever since.

In his book, David writes about the negative impacts CAFOs have on the quality of life of the people in his area of the state. In fact, CAFOs are the epitome of industrialization of agriculture, which degrade the rural environment, depress the rural economy, and tear the social fabric of rural communities asunder. To me, CAFOs are a clear and present threat to the sustainability of American agriculture. David mentions sustainable agriculture only a few times in his book, but I will always associate him with the sustainable agriculture movement. Reading his book does nothing to dispel this linkage in my mind. When David is writing about his experiences while living and working in rural North Missouri, including his interactions within the Amish community, he is giving a first-hand account of the sustainable agriculture movement in North Missouri.

In the early parts of the book, he tells stories of good people who left North Missouri after growing weary of the CAFO wars. As is clear in the book, this was at least one reason he and Alice decided to abandon their grass-based beef operation on the family farm and seek their future on a much smaller piece of land above a scenic valley in a nearby Amish farming community. They were rejecting the industrial paradigm of agriculture. They consciously chose an occupation and a lifestyle that could be achieved only through a more diversified, ecologically and socially sustainable approach to farming and living.

In more general terms, the book tells an interesting and insightful story of a young couple seeking a simpler life, more socially and spiritually rewarding way of living –*simply the greatest life*. This book is written as a series of stories about people, places, and both professional and personal experiences. Together they tell a story of the search for a better way of life.

David writes about their various experiences in choosing the perfect site for their new house and in constructing it of straw bales to function with maximum energy efficiency – "off the grid." Their choices of a floor plan, building materials, construction methods, were obviously motivated by a desire to live in harmony both with nature and with their new community.

Everything that is of any use to us comes either from nature or society. To the extent that we compromise the integrity of nature or society, we compromise the sustainability of human life on earth. A life of harmony is a life of sustainability. A life of harmony is also a life of peace and contentment at the core of our being, a life of true happiness and well-being. I am not sure if David and Alice thought of their life in these specific terms, but their desire to live *simply the greatest life* was a desire to live sustainably.

David also writes extensively about their life among the Amish families of their community. He emphasizes the priority Amish culture places on family and community. Amish families tend to be large and closely interconnected, both within and among families. Their chosen occupations and means of carrying out their work are designed specifically to provide learning experiences for their children, including the sense of being useful that comes from hard work.

Major business decisions are made with consideration of their impact on the future of the community. Economic enterprises that provide opportunities for people to work together are given priority over those that might make individuals more independent. While few of us in the so-called English community would choose a totally Amish way of life, the Amish exemplify the most fundamental principles of social connectedness that will be necessary to create sustainable communities and sustainable societies for the future.

David closes his book with four chapters that are philosophical as well as personal. He writes about the people whose philosophies have most influenced his life – "the trackers." He shares the experiences he and Alice have shared in their attempts to touch and stay in touch with their inner feelings – "the sweat lodge and vision quest." This was their way of searching for purpose and meaning in life – something we all seek by one means or another. Without purpose, life would have no meaning. Whatever we did would be neither good nor bad, neither right nor wrong. Too often too many of us become so distracted by the day to day concerns of making a living that we fail to stop and take stock of who we really are and what purpose we were meant to serve here on earth.

Without purpose, there would be no reason to choose a simpler life or a more sustainable lifestyle. There would be no way to define or even recognize when we were living the greatest life. *Our* greatest life is the life *we* were meant to live – our unique life of purpose. Our common sense tells us that our purpose is not to degrade and pollute the earth or to tear our communities asunder in our pursuit of economic self-interests. We were meant to care for the earth and to care for each other as we care for ourselves. We are meant to do these things in our own unique ways because we each have a unique contribution to make to the good of the greater whole.

We can never be sure that we are living our purpose or that we are walking the path we were meant to walk through life. Purpose cannot be found through logic or reason. We must rely instead on our insights, instincts, and intuition – the deeper spiritual dimension of self. As David reveals in the last chapter of his book, this spiritual quest to discover our true self may lead us in some unexpected directions.

# INTRODUCTION

HOMESTEADING OUR "OFF-THE-EVERYTHING" house seven life-altering miles from the security of the family farm had all the elements of a high-wire act without a net: Fear, excitement, possible disaster, and, ultimately, the exhilaration and validation of spectacular success. Only one rule applied to all aspects of our new farm, new home and new lives. Keep it simple.

The steady example of the Jamesport Amish community nourishes and inspires daily. Our green home - especially its unique marriage of stone and straw, my chicken plucker 'business from Heaven,' Alice's incredible horse operation – key features of our new lives – stitched together effortlessly within the solid quilt frame of this faith-based community.

In a decade of deliberate, simple country living, our fortified sense of place, our persistent soul searching, and the example and support of our Amish friends have taken us to surprising new inner frontiers.

Simplicity requires intention, deliberate assessment and constant re-evaluation. But the reward is no less than access to the magic and power of our deeper selves and unimaginable personal fulfillment.

Thank you for sharing this journey.

# PROLOGUE

Here's what has happened in the past 48 hours. Alice and I took topographical and plat maps to a site we had chosen from looking at them. We found a meadow running east-west with a house site on a southern slope. It is on the north edge of the south fork of Gees Creek and owned by an Amish man. There is no electricity, water, or phone line and the road is dirt. Across Gees Creek is the northern edge of 6000-acre Poosey Conservation Area – one of the last sites of Indian settlement in Missouri.

At the meadow we found running water and three to four acres of bottom land with a hawk gently gliding over the tall grass. Last night, after dinner at Luke and Marilyn's, Marilyn gave me this "Green House" journal and Les mentioned house-construction classes at NCMC.

This morning, Ab Yoder, our Amish friend who had moved to Michigan several years ago, called up to say he was moving back to Jamesport – to the Beechy Farm, not far from our site. Oh yes, and on the way to the meadow we passed an Amish church at Menno Graber's, the nearest house to our site.

Alice says these are all signs. And I'm having a hard time trying not to get excited with her.

# CHAPTER 1
# BARGAINING FOR PARADISE

"CAN YOU GIVE me a hand?" the young Amish man hailed from the gate. "I've got a chainsaw stuck in a burning tree!"

We nodded a shocked yes from our car and watched him open the gate, hop back into his buggy, and race across the farm. That explained the mystery of the racing buggy we'd been following, but a chain saw stuck in a burning tree? That was more mysterious. We followed at top buggy speed, taking in everything we could about this farm, part of which we hoped to buy.

When we crested a hill, everything suddenly turned black in front of us. The pastures had burned and so had part of the woods. The buggy wheels left parallel lines in the burnt grass pointing toward the mysterious chainsaw and burning tree somewhere in the distance.

Once again, we were astounded at the timing.

The first time Alice and I had come to see this property, three months earlier, the nearest Amish neighbors, the Menno Graber family, were having church in their home. Buggies and horses lined the little gravel road and the strong, pious singing that rose out of the dwelling set a reverential tone. Each Amish home hosts a church meeting about twice a year and we just happened upon this one at the Graber's – the first we had ever seen – as we drove to this property, this sacred land, to check it out.

Our visit to meet Norman to see if he might be interested in selling some land already had us charged with emotion. How often do you approach a complete stranger and just ask if they'd like to sell some property? Well, I guess he wasn't a complete stranger; we knew some of his relatives. But we were still a little uncertain about what Ernie Kauffman had told us.

"Norman is a bit unstable but settling down," he said.

"What do you mean 'unstable?'" we asked nervously.

Ernie laughed his gentle laugh, seeing that our minds had sped off in the wrong direction. "I just mean he's young and unmarried and not really established in the community yet."

Alice and I were always eager to learn more about these people who placed such a high value on community. So, unstable referred to Norman's place in the community. Well, there's probably an unstable period in nearly every young person's life, I had thought at the time. But as I took in the speeding buggy, burnt pastures, and prospect of chainsaw and burning tree, I couldn't help wonder if there was more to this 'unstable' Norman than Ernie let on.

Ernie was our best friend among the Amish and he had offered, exactly one month earlier, to introduce us to Norman some time. It was all we could do to let a month go by, but we thought it would seem overly eager to meet Norman any sooner. Now here we were, accompanied by Ernie, coming on the day Norman's property somehow caught on fire. And arriving, in fact, at the exact moment that he was riding into his property to tangle with a chainsaw and burning tree, needing help.

The buggy stopped at the corner of the pasture and Norman jumped out with a chainsaw in hand – one he had just borrowed from Menno Graber, as it turned out. We followed him into the woods. The fire had been put out by the Jamesport Rural Fire Department after only a short intrusion into the woods, but, sure enough, right on the edge of the fire line there stood one old tree with fire in it. If it fell in the wrong direction or dropped a burning limb the fire would start up again. With the firefighters gone, Norman had been cutting the tree down and trying to make it fall into the burned area. This was not necessarily the way the tree wanted to fall and it had rocked back onto his chain saw, pinching it in a wooden vice.

Only another chain saw could get it out, so Norman had sped to his nearest neighbor to borrow one and that's where we picked up the adventure.

Norman began to cut on the other side of the tree while Ernie held the pinched saw, ready to quickly pull it out and skedaddle when the tree fell. Alice and I watched the dangerous drama from a respectful distance. Either of them could be badly hurt or killed; falling trees have killed or severely injured several people we know. Alice and I confirmed later we had been thinking the same thought: that we might soon be talking to someone else about buying this property!

I felt sympathy for Norman. I knew all too well what he had gone through this afternoon. About ten years earlier, I had caught a large pasture on fire while burning leftover piles of hay – probably what Norman had been doing. I left thinking the fire couldn't spread. A little later I saw fire engines and pickups racing into that pasture. Our neighbor, Mickey, had called the fire department and it was a good thing he had. Dry grass had caught fire and taken it to the edge of the woods. The fire crew put it out there but it could have burned a lot of woods. That incident had given me quite a lot to think about.

Later, at Mickey's urging, Alice and I joined the Grundy Country Rural Fire Department and trained and fought many fires with them. Mickey was ex-Navy and versed in fire fighting. We helped raise money for equipment; we trained with the Trenton Fire Department, even going inside burning houses. We had experienced many house and barn and grass fires and knew how exhausting it was to fight them all. One of our fellow GCRFD members, Gary King, had a heart attack and died while fighting a fire. We took it seriously.

Branches fell around Ernie and Norman as the tree rocked and the chainsaw whined. Seeing the right moment, Ernie pulled the pinched saw out and retreated to safety. Down came the tree with a crash onto the blackened forest floor. We doused the tree with water from a back pack left by the Jamesport Rural Fire Department until we were satisfied that all danger was past.

"Norman, this is David and Alice," Ernie finally had a chance to introduce us.

"Just why are you here now?" Norman asked. "I can't believe your timing."

"Well," I said, kicking dirt and launching into a version of my prepared speech, "Alice and I have farmed on my grandparent's place about eight miles north of here for twenty years." I felt sorry for this young man, knowing he was exhausted, maybe a little embarrassed and perhaps even disgusted. I certainly didn't want to take advantage of him at a time like this. Proposing a purchase offer to someone in his condition just didn't seem fair. But here we were so I continued.

"And we were thinking it'd be nice to have a place of our own...."

There's no way I could have told him about the topographical map that I ordered and Alice drawing a circle on part of his property because it combined our three desires: near Poosey Conservation Area; having a creek beneath a south-facing slope; and being close to the Amish community. There's no way I could or would have told him Alice had started jumping up and down and yelling, "That's it! That's it! I know that's the place!"

I would have been crazy to tell him about all the signs we considered as proof this was to be our place: that first drive past Menno's church; our walk down the muddy road, lined with towering trees; the creek water flowing ice-free in some spots; and the beautiful meadow along the creek – the land features Alice had searched for; and, finally, the red-tailed hawk that glided across the meadow as we stood at the edge.

"And we liked the idea of being close to the conservation area and this property seemed to fit..." I trailed off. There was so much I couldn't tell Norman, but I didn't have to.

He got it all instantly.

"Yeah, I know just how you feel," he took over. "I said the same thing to Paul Troyer three years ago." Our hearts sank.

"I told Paul if he ever wanted to sell to give me the first chance at it."

Just as I'd feared – he had an emotional attachment to the land. There's no way he'd sell an acre of it. We'd convinced ourselves we'd been seeing signs, we'd worked up the nerve to approach this fellow and now we were certainly the fools. Both Alice and I felt ourselves drop to the pit of despair.

"About how many acres were you thinking of?" he asked.

You could have knocked us over with a feather!

"Oh, forty. Or sixty. You know, just enough for a little farm."

"Well, as a matter of fact, I have been thinking about building log houses out here and selling some properties. I've got several people interested already."

I soon realized that any time I'd spent feeling like I might take advantage of Norman was time wasted. Norman was sharp as a tack and could look out for himself. And so began the bargaining process that was to carry on for several weeks and make nervous wrecks out of all three of us.

Now I'll admit straight away I'm no bargainer. I'd rather give the other person the deal and be a nice guy and make no waves. Not Alice. Alice was raised in South America where there is no such thing as a fixed price. She had bargaining in her blood and loved the game. I can't count the times I've been embarrassed to the point of walking away by Alice's penchant for haggling. She knows all the tricks and is a grand master at the game.

And she doesn't limit her bargaining to outdoor markets. In shopping malls she'll find a lovely article of clothing and then see the loose button, bad hem, or pulled thread.

I'll then cringe and do my invisibility routine while Alice marches up to the clerk to claim her bargain.

Once in the local Hy Vee grocery store, of all places, she got a hanging plant reduced. I don't know which was reduced more, the hanging plant or me. I could barely stand it.

But when it came to selling bulls – our principle livelihood on the farm – I loved Alice's performances. Within fifteen minutes of the arrival of a prospective bull buyer, Alice would be slapping the breast pocket on their bib overalls and crying out something like, "Why Herbert, you know that's cheap for a bull like that!"

Getting slapped playfully by a cute young woman with the sales intensity of an Arab merchant was both disorienting and disarming. Our breeding program was pretty solid, too, but I attribute our high sales per visit rate to Alice's intensity on the hunt.

My dad witnessed one of Alice's performances when a bull buyer came to the farm and, having a temperament more like mine, he was aghast at her tactics. "Those boys never had a chance," he reported to the family. "She turned their pockets inside out."

At cajoling, wheedling, and general convincing, Alice was the best I'd seen. Once again, I pitied Norman for what he was about to go through. And once again, Norman surprised me.

Norman is gifted with a sharp, analytical mind and is willing to fight hard for his best price. I never thought I'd see it but Alice had met her match. The two went at it like pit bulls and I was stuck in the pit with them. I would rather have taken a beating.

Between rounds, I pleaded with Alice to back off a little. I was afraid the whole deal would be ruined, but Alice had a good feel for how hard she could push. She knew Norman wanted to sell. But Norman also knew how badly we wanted to buy! The gap between ask and offer was way too wide and after several weeks we just weren't getting anywhere.

Since Norman, like all Jamesport Amish, had no phone in the house, he would call us from a phone box near his farm. Sometimes we were in, sometimes not. We couldn't call him back. It was very frustrating for all of us. We finally set up an evening meeting at Norman's house.

It was awkward. Alice and Norman did most of the talking; I was out of their league and they both knew it. They were focused on the per-acre price. The exact number of acres in question had yet to be determined.

Each had a new twist to try to tip the scales in their direction. Each spoke at length but nobody budged. After what seemed an eternity to me, I sensed we were reaching a critical, make-or-break-the-deal, moment. Then three things happened nearly simultaneously.

Norman had been waiting for the veterinarian to show up to look at a newborn colt that was very weak. We heard Dr. Dan's pickup roll in and head for the barn. Any time a farmer calls a vet it is serious business and you don't want to waste a vet's time. Norman had to leave.

But before Norman could go, Menno Graber knocked on the door. It was dark outside. Menno is 6' 5" tall, thin, and with prominent cheekbones. I'd never seen him before but with his stature and the cut of his beard, I swore I was looking at Abe Lincoln. He had come to retrieve his chain saw.

Impulsively I said to Norman before he could respond to either, "Would you take $55,000 for the east 70 acres today?" Time froze for three seconds. I was focused on Norman, who was quickly calculating the new tack, but I knew what was going to happen with Alice. Alice and I had agreed beforehand what our range was. It was not part of the deal for me to step in with an offer we hadn't discussed. As I knew she would, Alice stormed out of Norman's house mad as a hornet. Norman knew he had found the top edge of our gray area.

"Can you promise me you'll give that price?" Norman was really asking if I was sure I could talk Alice into it.

"I think so."

He thought another second, said he'd let me know in two days and left for the colt and the chain-saw.

I walked to the car and got the tongue-lashing I deserved. It was an outrageously high price I'd offered, closer to Norman's than ours. Alice was hurt that I hadn't consulted her nor allowed the bargaining process to unfold.

But I was sick of bickering and afraid Norman was getting sick of us not budging. The gap between his price and ours was too big and not moving.

Alice was certain Norman would come down but I didn't want to lose the deal. I also knew that the dramatic scene from my offer would let Norman know he probably wasn't going to do better from us.

Neither Alice nor I slept much that night.

---

**Green House Journal – Entry #10, May 4, 1997**

*On the evening of May 1 we drove out there and walked in from Ray Harris's land. We looked at Ab Yoder's old place – possibly to rent. We went down to the bottoms to step off 880 paces to see where the '80-line' came down. The valley was gorgeous, and a hawk – probably the same hawk we saw on our first trip there – flew over and called twice. Alice generously said we ought to buy this land at any price. We made up and had a wonderful evening.*

---

The next morning, Alice's birthday, Norman called and we arranged a meeting. Alice flew to Ukiah, California to attend a workshop on solar energy. I met Norman at an abstract company in Trenton and signed a contract. It looked like the paradise we had bargained for was going to be ours.

# Chapter 2
# The Ideal Location

O UR FIRST PROPERTY walks invariably included tromps through the brush and around the trees where we had decided the house should be sited - on the slope overlooking the magic meadow. The exposure was ideal: due south, and nestled into the woods with a great view.

Magnificent oaks, hickories, maples, cottonwoods, walnuts and sycamores lined the long, narrow meadow and surrounded the site. The far side of the meadow was bordered by a meandering dirt road, the county line. On the other side of the road, Gees Creek happily carved away at the eighty-foot high, tree-lined bluff of the north edge of the Poosey Conservation Area. It was idyllic.

We walked the site many times with family and friends. One glorious evening at sunset we walked in with our dear friends Les and Denise Turner, fellow refugees from a fierce and futile battle to keep corporate hog farms out of our area. A whippoorwill started his non-stop nocturnal call to the delight of Alice's and my ears. Les, perhaps hardened by corporate hog neighbors with a smell that wouldn't quit day or night, said, "Those dad-gum things will do that all night long!"

Alice and I loved the bird song and everything else about the site and ignored the cautious observations of more knowledgeable folks like Les, my Dad, and Alice's brother Bill, who all have practical experience with construction and engineering and noted some of the challenges of the site. Heck, it was ideal!

Well, there were a few considerations that were less than ideal and eventually we had to face them. The driveway would be handy to the road but pretty steep to the house. We would have to remove some of the big trees. We would have to excavate back into the hillside and the limestone outcrops sprinkled along the hill promised a challenge. The house would be plainly visible from the road in the winter when the leaves were gone. Speaking of leaves, boy would we have a gutter full in the fall! Situated on the south end of the property, we were distant from all the pastures where the stock would be grazing so chores would always begin with a hearty walk up the steep hill.

Whew! What about mosquitoes down in the valley? And would it be muggy in the summer? As doubt (and a smidgen of practicality) crept in, our minds opened to the rest of the farm and suddenly new information flooded in.

Christopher Alexander, in his book <u>A Pattern Language</u>, recommends leaving the property's best spots undisturbed. He also recommends locating in the center of the property for privacy as well as better accessibility to the rest of the property. Alice's Aunt Phyllis, not having seen the place, but knowing some of its features, said, "Why not put the house overlooking the pond like Emmy and Bill's place? That's so beautiful."

Hmmm, house in the center? Overlooking the pond…? We walked into the center of the property and looked down at the little pond bordering the woods. It was a beautiful site. We stood in a fence line, overgrown with brush and small trees. The trees provided a safe wildlife corridor from woods on one side of the property to woods on the other. To the northwest was a thick stand of young hickories to keep the cold wind and snow of winter at bay.

Directly in front of us was a very healthy pasture we called "mouse city" because you couldn't walk fifty yards into it without seeing at least one mouse. This might not put it on the "plus" side of the ledger for most folks, but to nature crazy people like us it was a larder for hawks, owls, fox, and coyote and guaranteed some great field observations.

Alice and I stood near the high point of the property taking this all in. Not a house was in view from here. Not a light could be seen at night. We whispered to each other out of reverence for this land that had claimed us. It all came clear in an instant. This was the spot. It had all the features that were important and none of the hassles. We felt it and knew it to the core.

"Look!" Alice whispered pointing almost straight up. I followed her hand to a "vee" of geese and heard them encouraging each other like teammates. Creating an updraft for each other, each with a clear view toward some better future, geese were the ideal symbol for cooperation and empowerment of each other. Mates for life on a quest to lands scarcely imaginable, they flew directly along the fence line, directly along the path of trees and directly over our future home like a divine pointer as if to say, "Here it is! Here is the ideal location!"

And as they flew on west to who-knows-where our spirits soared with them.

# CHAPTER 3
# PLAN A: TIMBER FRAME HOME

THE WAY WE decided what kind of house we wanted was pretty much the same way our bull customers decided what kind of bull they wanted. Whatever was worst with the last one was what they didn't want with the new one. This time they wanted one without horns, or a black one, or one that sired smaller calves, or bigger calves.

This time we wanted a house with electric outlets where we needed them. Doors that shut and latched. A metal roof that would never leak or need new shingles. We wanted windows that didn't rattle in a breeze. We wanted walls that were warm to the touch and a floor that we never had to crawl under to tack up insulation.

We wanted a simple sewage system that never backed up, fences requiring no paint, and a lawn the size of a postage stamp. We wanted lots of closet space, a bath tub, and some privacy. We wanted to be warm in the winter and cool in the summer.

We wanted a turn-around driveway and to be on the least traveled gravel road in the county. We wanted the nearest neighbor to be half a mile away. That's not to say we didn't love Grandma and Grandpa's farm and our "quaint" old farm house. It had to have been fantastic in other ways for us to put up with the living conditions and endless maintenance.

Intoxicated by all the amenities of our future dream home, I thought I was Superman and decided I'd build it with hand tools the old way – with hand-hewn mortise and tenon joints.

The intoxication lasted several months. I read books and even spent a week in the Smoky Mountains of South Carolina as a timber frame apprentice. In a freezing cold shop heated only by portable propane furnaces, half a dozen apprentices like me and a few old hands sawed, drilled and carved away at the joints on pine timbers for a house kit.

All our measurements and markings had to be approved by the old hands before we actually cut and drilled. Still the boss-man told us that one of us would screw up around the middle of the week. How did he know?

On Wednesday I was trying to figure out a complicated peak joint at the end of a huge timber that had all the other joints finished in it. There was a lot of pencil drawing at the end and I wanted to figure it out before I cut. The boss-man came by and caught me just staring at the joint and gave me a verbal giddy-yup in no uncertain terms. After all he was trading training for labor and he'd had his share of free-loaders hanging around without working much.

I picked up the big circular saw and cut off the wrong piece of a twenty-foot timber that already had about thirty man-hours of work in it. Boss-man saw the disaster and passed a kidney stone. I was reminded how much I enjoyed working for myself.

Like all disasters, that one turned out to be not nearly so bad. I made instant friends with all the slackers and boss-haters. And one of the old hands saved the day by joining a new peak end onto the twenty-foot timber.

I went home with a great love for timber frame homes and the Smoky Mountains and a renewed commitment to be the boss-man, and I lovingly drafted a set of my very own house plans.

There is something deeply comforting about visible timbers in a home. They represent strength, stability, simplicity and old-world style. Their hidden joints speak of depth, craftsmanship and elegant engineering. The rough hewn wood connects us back to nature. I pored over my plans, refining, detailing the joints, figuring the dimensions and loads, and tallying the timbers needed.

We harvested our first trailer load of mature, straight oaks from the 250 acres of woods on the old farm and took them to Joni Beechy's sawmill in Jamesport. Joni's sawmill, like the other five or six sawmills in the area, was set up to cut pallet lumber, that is, lumber that goes a mile down the road to a pallet shop where some teenage Amish boys with air-powered nail guns slap them together at lightening speed. They load a semi full and a driver delivers the rig.

We just thought a sawmill was a sawmill open for business from anyone and naïvely we asked Joni to do our specialty work.

We'd had some connections with the Beechys. One of Joni's daughters, Rosemary, assisted Grandma at her home once a week, the only Amish gal in Grandma's crew. Rosemary's ready smile and delightfully direct personality made her a joy to be around.

Plus, just a year earlier, after we had harvested some walnut with Alice's folks, Ted and Nancy, Joni had turned it into some beautiful planks. Ted and Nancy had studied furniture making and crafted some lovely chairs and tables over the years, including some beautiful pieces out of this walnut.

At that earlier visit to Joni's with Ted and Nancy there were a few moments of uncertainty.

I now realize that Joni's crew of six or seven guys were probably all paid by the board-foot, and used to working at full speed, so when we showed up with our dinky little walnut logs and Joni agreed to cut them for us, those boys all got a non-union, non-paying break courtesy of us.

Using a team of telepathic horses, Leon Troyer pulled the logs off our truck. Joni loaded them onto the tracks that fed into his giant saw.

Joni cast a practiced eye up and down the logs looking for tell-tale nail scars. One big spike run through a sawmill blade can ruin the day for a sawyer and his crew.

Anyway, we told Joni what we wanted and he began cutting. First the bark came off, then a few edge pieces with a little wane in them, and then the prime interior wood was cut up. Joni didn't rush. He rotated the log several times, sizing it up for the best cuts. The wood squirted off onto a roller table and the boys stacked it neatly.

The second log was handled in the same way. We brought the truck around to the open end of the sawmill and stacked the beautiful dark, rich-smelling boards in the truck bed, Ted and Nancy just about jumping up and down with excitement. To actually be a part of the entire process of furniture making all the way back to felling the tree and watching the raw boards get sawed out is a rare treat. Good walnut lumber was not cheap and Ted and Nancy knew it.

Ted walked over to Joni to settle up. Joni pulled a receipt pad out of his little office and wrote some numbers down and handed the sheet to Ted. The rest of us watched from a distance as Ted stared at the bill for some time. Finally he wrote out a check and we thanked Joni and said our goodbyes.

We had been speculating what the cost would be since we hadn't discussed it beforehand. Then Ted showed us the bill. It simply had $1500 on it with the zeros in the cents column. Ted had pondered for quite some time whether it really was only fifteen dollars or fifteen hundred dollars! Fifteen was how it was written. But fifteen dollars?! We should have given Joni more.

Here I was, a few years later, and I still hadn't realized what an imposition it was and how much higher Joni's bill should have been. I asked him if he'd be willing to cut 8 x 8-inch and 4 x 4-inch timbers out of some oak logs.

"I just wonder if I can cut it accurate enough for you," Joni said in a friendly way. Today I would read that as, "David, we really don't do this type of thing," but not back then.

"Oh sure you can," I said without a clue. "I can make it work if it's a little off." Another fantasy.

Joni probably would have preferred to pass this "opportunity" along to someone else but I didn't give him a chance so he agreed to cut the timbers in a few days.

That Saturday morning our timbers were ready to pick up at Joni's. Before leaving to fetch them, I checked in at Grandma's house, which we jokingly referred to as the "master's house," our little house next door being the slaves' quarters, of course. Clara George was with Grandma on Saturdays. Clara was the field general of all the gals that came in to help Grandma. She coordinated the crew, spending untold hours on the phone to make sure Grandma was cared for.

Grandma was in and out of the hospital with every ailment you can imagine. But Grandma was one of those rare people who were just too tough to let go. She endured more bodily break-down than anyone I've ever known and kept plodding on through it all. My Great Aunt Wuanita nicknamed Grandma the "Mighty Midget" (she was barely five feet tall) back in the 1930s and it was, if anything, even more appropriate sixty years later.

Some people wondered if Grandma's toughness wasn't due to the slow starvation and general deprivation she had endured for three years as a prisoner of war, finally liberated in 1945 and weighing only 69 pounds. Maybe it was, but I was less charitable and attributed it to a flat out stubborn personality. She could've worn down a mule in a pulling contest.

She sure wore me down and Alice will tell you I have plenty of that "mule" gene in me. As far as I was concerned Clara and all the gals that helped her deserved congressional medals of honor and free lifetime psychiatric treatment.

Clara was her usual upbeat and thoughtful self that Saturday and handed me a clipping from the morning's Kansas City Star. Alice and I hadn't taken newspapers and hardly turned on the radio since our bitter year fighting corporate hog farms so we were always glad when someone connected to the outside world shared news with us, especially good news.

The story was about a couple an hour away in Lathrop, Missouri, who had built their own straw bale home. "I just thought you kids might be interested in it," Clara said.

I thanked her and read the clipping with mild interest. Alice read it too.

"Let's call Les and Denise and see if they want to see the straw bale home," she suggested on a lark. We called the Turners and made a plan to meet right after picking up the logs at Joni's.

# CHAPTER 4
# FROM GIANT HOGS TO THREE
# LITTLE PIGS

As Les and Denise and Alice and I drove together to see the straw-bale house, conversation ranged from the latest depressing corporate hog farm news to the fun we had with our pastured-poultry operations. Les and Denise were perfect comrades to share dreams of a better future.

Despite our efforts of the past few years to prevent it, a brand new battery of hog sheds – only one installation of many throughout the area – had just been erected across the road from Les and Denise's farm home. We had talked to other corporate hog-farm neighbors in north Missouri and North Carolina and not one was happy about it. Many felt their lives were in shambles because their properties were useless for outdoor activity and their health was jeopardized by airborne contaminants. The stench was overwhelming and unavoidable; respiratory and headache problems were well documented.

Les and Denise and a large group of neighbors had lost the battle to stop the construction but fought on to shut down the operations on the grounds that Continental Grain violated the statutes in Missouri that strictly prohibited large corporate ownership of livestock facilities. In fact, that's how we met Les and Denise back in 1994 at the first NALSO meeting.

NALSO, Neighbors Against Large Swine Operations, was an unfortunately negative name. Causes should always be for something. Perhaps the name cursed the group and limited its success. Though NALSO eventually won large law suits in Missouri and pioneered anti-hog activism in the Midwest, the general feeling was always one of defeat because the giant hog factories got in and stayed in.

It was a David and Goliath story. Except this giant was a giant hog and impossible to hit. We hurled stone after stone but had no good targets. We never even saw the phantom "family farm" owners who lived in New York and had layers and layers of underlings between them and the ground floor of their investment schemes.

We threw stones at the state governmental agencies that slept in Jefferson City while the corporate reapers snuck in to north Missouri. A few blinked; most looked the other way. We threw stones at our local legislators who courted the disaster and helped sneak the giant hogs in. There we landed some solid blows but the results were counter productive. Most of our stones went willy-nilly off into the air, serving only to relieve a tiny bit of the incredible frustration we felt.

It's a funny thing, but once a huge business like this has established a physical presence and has operations up and going and is paying salaries and taxes and pounding its chest in the local papers, well, it's impossible to rally anybody against it no matter how illegal, polluting, unhealthy, dishonest, economically questionable, or amoral it is. Nobody wants to listen.

The corporate hog boys know this and count on it. The first raiders that snuck into Missouri were Premium Standard Farms. Kicked out of Iowa in no uncertain terms, they got the last laugh by locating, via legislation exempting three north Missouri counties from the corporate farm law, right on the Iowa line, stinking up the state anyway.

Premium Standard Farms (PSF) was a shell game, a Ponzi scheme that snookered a few dozen well-heeled investors. So breathless was PSF's rush to establish a physical presence that they offered unimaginable wages to the Amish carpenters who left home in van loads to build hog barn after hog barn. Amishmen told of pouring cement in sub-zero temperatures, knowing full well it wouldn't cure properly or last long, but that's what they were told to do. Electricians reported the unheard-of practice of wiring buildings without blueprints.

Big shots from all over the world were flown in on Lear jets and shuttled from installation to installation. They were dazzled by this empire in the making and signed on at $10 million each! The initial deal raised $330 million and "guaranteed" a 30% payback to begin after seven years.

A few months before the seven-year payback was to begin, and exactly as NALSO had predicted, PSF filed for bankruptcy (due, they said, to low hog prices). The big investors took a big hit, the PSF top dogs faded away with fat savings accounts, and Continental Grain bought the facilities for ten cents on the dollar, probably still too high.

The PSF boys were amateur scammers compared to Continental Grain. Continental Grain didn't sneak, didn't tamper with legislation, and didn't site facilities so as to thumb their nose at anyone. They waltzed in smiling, just like they owned the place, as if deserving a standing ovation. And do you know what happened? People began clapping! Then they stood! And they cheered!

We watched in mute horror as the local paper printed a front page picture of smiling people canoeing on a new hog "lagoon!" Never mind that in three months that "lagoon" would be a cesspool containing hundreds of thousands of gallons of acrid hog crap and urine with the ghostly jellyfish of afterbirth floating on its scummy surface. You wouldn't want to get close enough to photograph that "lagoon" with a three-foot lens, let alone put a canoe in it.

Never mind that Continental Grain had neither a plan nor a care in the world for what might happen to those dozens of incredibly concentrated cesspools should they decide to invest in Dutch tulips next year and pack their Missouri bags. Never mind the toxic concentration of chemicals and nutrients they would spray on nearby crop fields to disperse the by-product of their factory system. Never mind the poor souls downwind.

Main Street was in love with Continental Grain, the local newspaper was starry-eyed, absolutely tripping over itself to heap praise. But those starry eyes turned blood-shot when NALSO wanted to debate the issue in print.

At the very first public talk by a Continental Grain representative, NALSO orchestrated a protest in which 125 placard-carrying and chanting anti-hog folks in the school parking lot laid down their signs, walked into the school auditorium and silently took places along the walls, registering protest by refusing to be seated. The next day's Republican Times headlines read: "Standing Room Only Crowd Attends Continental Grain Talk."

That's what we were up against from the start. It went downhill from there. Soon the paper refused to sell NALSO advertising space. Frustration levels soared and, in hindsight, it is truly remarkable that no property was damaged and no one was hurt.

Oh, there were a few little things like dancing survey stakes and unyielding snow plows and phone threats – so we heard. The hope for legal victory channeled most of the pent up energy, but one notable and hilarious – to us, anyway – act of guerrilla warfare stood out.

The local legislator was the easiest target. He lived here; he was accountable. He had assisted both PSF and Continental Grain and from our viewpoint had opened a huge can of worms in order to gain local jobs at the expense of real farmers.

The legislator's popular annual fund raiser for years had been a golf tournament at the Gallatin golf course. A beautiful dawn welcomed the faithful and they teed off happily, probably telling jokes and swapping good-natured lies like golfers do. All must have been rosy until the flag was pulled on the first green.

It came up dripping and reeking. With tears in our eyes we imagined the first foursome crowded around, bending over slightly, sniffing and gagging and feeling our legislator's pain.

It wasn't the first, and far from the last, instance of hog wastes getting out of bounds. PSF had already had several major spills and downstream fish kills. That darn stuff was just looking for ways to get out.

Somehow, certainly, all the cups were emptied of "lagoon water" though the smell had to remain and taint every falling ball. The "gimme" allowance probably extended generously that morning after the infamous "night the pigs flew."

Other than that, we had very little to laugh about. People's lives were turned upside down: good friends found themselves on opposite sides of the fence and no longer spoke to each other; cattle and people became extremely ill. Some people sold their farms and moved away in disgust and defeat. Legal battles plodded on to the advantage of no one but the lawyers.

The complexity and negativity of the story make it difficult and unpleasant to tell. A year embroiled in negativity with no one listening and no one helping or caring tied me in knots of frustration. I so much wanted a better rural life for people.

That was the purpose of the Green Hills Farm Project, a grazer's group we started in 1988. That's why we shared our farm and our insights with grazing schools and at conferences around the country and in magazine articles. The agriculture we espoused was small scale, pasture-based, environmentally enhancing, aromatically pleasing, aesthetic, and non-threatening.

Our legislator had been our champion only a few years earlier when he spearheaded legislation to encourage sustainable agriculture. Unfortunately we forgot about that when corporate farming invaded our back yard. Our model and the Wall Street model were worlds apart with virtually no common ground.

I failed to see the irony or hypocrisy in being a proponent for a higher quality of life on the one hand and eternally negative about the giant hog farms on the other. My quality of life was in the manure pits and Alice, who misses little and ignores less, called me on it one evening.

"Are you really happy?"

Well, what kind of a question was that? But right away I knew it could not be shrugged off. Not with Alice.

"On the whole, no. I feel like I have responsibilities that never ease up, that the work will never be done. Plus, we've lived in the same tiny house for fifteen years…it feels like a rut."

We both knew a rut was just a grave with the ends knocked out. Then came the life-changing question.

"What would it take for you to be happy?"

"I don't want to work so hard," I said.

"Okay," Alice coached, "but put it in a positive statement."

"Well, I'd like to have fewer acres and fewer cattle to manage, no winter chores, no hay-making, no frozen waterers to deal with, no OB/GYN duties – in other words, no momma cows."

It was a ridiculous notion, impossible to conceive from where we stood. Alice guided me forward, ignoring my negativity.

"Okay. Fewer cows and fewer acres. How many?"

"Just enough to survive with the meat business…30 or 40 acres and 15 or 20 head of cattle. And some sheep, of course."

"How many?"

"Oh…40…50…60. And pigs and chickens, too. But no purebred business."

A preposterous thought! The purebred cattle business was our bread and butter and we had worked hard at developing superior breeding stock adapted to pasture alone, no grain feeding.

Yet I was willing to give that up to gain peace of mind.

My negativity over the hog situation finally forced me – with Alice's help – to face the things I didn't like in this world of my own creation! What an incredible gift those giant hogs gave me! How ungrateful I had been! Would I have ever come to that reckoning on my own? I have to wonder.

From that moment on we played the game of imagining our perfect farm operation, our perfect house, our perfect life.

The land features were simple: 40 to 60 acres with at least 30 in pasture; well laid-out permanent pastures that were easily subdivided with electric fence; many watering points from an efficient, clean water source; some woods; and a nice house.

It was the house that ended up getting most of our focus. I guess we never let ourselves realize how much we despised the tiny farmhouse we'd called home for so long. Our new home would be everything that one wasn't: efficient, roomy, attractive, and earth friendly.

Soon we had convinced ourselves that Grandma and Grandpa's dream farm was not our dream farm and that we could make a living on our own. Like dominoes falling, things kept happening to help us on our way towards this exciting, new life.

Two big dominoes fell the morning we drove with Les and Denise to see the straw-bale home in Lathrop. The first was the straw-bale concept itself and Clara giving us the article about the folks in Lathrop. The second was our disappointment when we collected the timbers Joni cut at his sawmill. We knew Joni got as much out of those logs as anyone could have, but the pile of timbers was pitifully small. We'd have to cut down a lot of trees to build the house I designed.

The minute we walked into it, everything about Jerry and Joyce Tichener's straw-bale home appealed to us: The walls – almost two feet thick – had an adobe look and a soft pastel color. The luxurious window sills begged for potted plants and sun-napping cats. The air inside felt vibrant and pure.

Perhaps because they were in the business of building homes, Jerry and Joyce were willing hosts and forthcoming with information. Jerry's passion was to provide low cost/low maintenance housing. That passion led him to experiment with straw bales as an insulating material. We appreciated the fact that, as a contractor and businessman, Jerry chose to use straw bales strictly from a practical viewpoint, not an idealistic one.

We toured some of his other homes, one of which was under construction. As we learned more from Jerry about the cost of building materials, the alternative energy sources they used, and the ease of construction, our spirits rose with the exciting possibilities.

We quickly detached from the timber-frame home idea, my extensive plans now just a mental exercise, my apprenticeship in North Carolina just a week of vacation. Before the day was done, Jerry had agreed to pour our foundation and to be our consultant while we built our new straw-bale home.

While driving back, Les quipped that with a house made of straw we'd be right up there with the three little pigs. We shared a good laugh, not knowing we'd hear that line about a thousand more times in the next two years.

# CHAPTER 5
# A HOME OF STRAW, STICKS ...

ALICE AND I sat on lawn chairs in the large room that would some day be our kitchen. Eating the snacks we'd packed at the old farm and gazing out at the pond at the edge of the woods, we picked up the ongoing discussion that currently perplexed us: What material were we going to use to cover the straw bales on the outside of the house and how would we attach it?

It was not unusual for us to be approaching a big task without an answer at hand. The whole house up to this point had been built on instant decision changes inspired by chance encounters just like Clara telling us about the straw-bale home.

Without intending it, we had undertaken a task requiring more faith than we had ever been forced to muster. Neither of us were carpenters, although Alice had once helped build a house in her home construction class at North Central Missouri College. And even though Alice has one of the most absorbent minds you'll ever find, there were dozens of normal house construction decisions to make that we really didn't have a clue about. And dozens more arose because our house was so unconventional.

We milked Jerry Tichener for all we could. The arrangement was $1000 worth of meat for access to his knowledge. But as Jerry later said, "I would have been better off at a dollar a question!"

We apologized for inundating him with questions.

"It wouldn't be so bad if you did half the things I suggested," he followed up, only half in jest.

It was true. We followed Jerry's model to a point, then struck off in directions of our own. Jerry's streamlined process was to frame the house in a modified post-and-beam style with the window- and door-frame vertical members supporting the beam "header" around the circumference of the house.

The frame supports the house and the roof and is, itself, supported by a floating slab of concrete that thickens at the outside edges of the house. Anchored in the concrete at the edges are rebar rods protruding up three feet. Onto these, Jerry skewers his first two rows of straw bales in a one-over-two, two-over-one pattern like brick laying.

The straw bales continue up to the beam, each row "pinned" together with thin bamboo rods. Once the straw is in place, Jerry "sews" expanded metal lathe sheets (think of giant cheese graters) to both sides of the straw bales using homemade, two-foot long "needles" and baling wire as thread. The metal lathe sheets hold the cement plaster that Jerry and his crew trowel on next, both inside and outside the house.

We got as far as the metal lathe and I balked.

"I don't want to live in a house with two layers of metal in the walls," I told Alice.

"Well, why didn't you think of that before we drove to Kansas City and bought two pallets of metal lathe?"

It was a fair question. I remembered when we bought the lathe. Alice asked a few burly plaster workers about tricks of the trade. They made the whole process sound like Olympic training.

"Just try and hold eight pounds out in front of you all day long with one hand!" one bearded fellow challenged Alice. He looked like he could hold a piano out in front of him. Alice was a stick figure by comparison. We bought light aluminum mud holders and trowels, neither encouraged nor enlightened about plastering.

"I don't know why I didn't think of it before now, but it just doesn't feel right. I mean here we are in the middle of nature, not another house in sight. We have white oak posts from the old farm and straw bales from Mike Eckert's place down the road…it just doesn't feel right to put metal in the walls."

Alice, bless her heart, has zero tolerance for my bad ideas, but she has the utmost respect for my feelings. So I've learned I must use the word "feel" when I propose a new idea.

"Well then, we'll just have to find another way to put the plaster on," she decided with finality.

The magical answer came, within days, through our dear friend, Andy.

Andy, short for Andrea, and Ken, her boyfriend, were our personal house-building angels. For years we had secretly called Ken our "customer from Heaven," not because Ken is a master chef trained in one of the country's most prestigious culinary schools, nor because he had commanded the kitchens at the finest restaurants in Kansas City. We bestowed "Customer from Heaven" status on Ken because he has a walk-in freezer in his home!

We encourage customers to purchase deep chest freezers to better handle our seasonal meat production. Then they can place larger, more efficient orders, which we reward with a discounted price. Ken needed no such inspiration; he was far ahead of the curve. Ken's yearly order set records in every category: 50 chickens, two lambs, one whole hog, two turkeys, and half a beef. Now that's the kind of commitment that warms our hearts. (Okay, and our wallets, too!)

Not only is Ken a master chef, but we discovered, to our great surprise and delight, that he's also a master carpenter. Almost a year earlier, on a meat delivery, we had told Ken we were about to build our own house.

"Oh, really. Do you have good tools?" he asked.

"Like what?" we responded.

"Oh, nail guns, sheet rock equipment, stuff like that."

"No. We don't have nail guns," I said. "And I've never even heard of sheet rock equipment!"

Ken laughed, guided us down to his basement and introduced us to drywall cutting, holding, and lifting tools, nail guns of various calibers and a large assortment of other tools. We were wide-eyed with wonder.

"I thought you were a chef," I said in disbelief at his incredible tool collection.

"I used to finish houses, too," Ken said.

"No kidding!"

"Yes. I built this house."

"You built *this* house!?"

We were standing in a gorgeous 4500-square foot house built on five different levels with three full stairways, cut out ceilings, and very steep roofs with many gables. It had a full commercial kitchen in the basement (with the walk-in freezer). Had it been a meal it would have been a showcase, four-star meal for a party of twelve.

I began to see the pattern in Ken: Master the craft using the best tools of the trade. My estimation of him was rising faster than an Amish barn.

We heaped thousands of dollars worth of tools into our truck, effusive in our thanks and astonished at our good fortune. Beyond our meat transactions, we really didn't know Ken that well and here he was just giving his tools away.

"You know this could take us a long time, Ken. We're only going to be able to work a few hours a day on it."

"Don't worry," he said. "Just give them back when you're through with them."

The benefit of Ken's marvelous tools – huge as it was – was only the tip of the iceberg. Ken asked if we would like them to come up to help sometime.

"Are you kidding? We'll supply the fillets!"

So began a wonderful relationship built around our house construction, Ken and Andy's talent and generosity, and sumptuous feasts that we all pitched in on since all of us are dedicated "foodies."

Ken and Andy saw the house site before we broke ground. They helped put trusses, rafters and roof on. They helped place the first hundred straw bales. They helped build the raised floor of our library and assisted during several layers of the endless plastering on the inside. Jessica and Mason, Ken's kids, helped too, happily scampering into the rafters to place the liners that would keep the blow-in insulation from getting out over the eaves. Ken helped hang windows and frame doors.

The spirit of Ken and Andy's generosity is forever embedded in the house.

It was only a week after Ken and Andy had helped put in the first hundred straw bales that I balked on the metal lathe. Alice was on the phone to Andy telling her of the stalemate in development.

"David thinks there must be a more natural way than metal lathe," Alice told Andy.

"OH!" Andy's signature enthusiastic exclamation. "I know just who you should talk to. Cedar Rose in Silverthorne. She's a natural building materials consultant."

Only Andy-from-Aspen would know a natural building materials consultant. That afternoon we were on the phone with Cedar Rose Galbraith. When I asked if there were alternatives to metal lathe she said, "You don't want to use metal lathe. Which way are your bales facing? Are the strings up or on the side?"

"Our bales are wire-tied and the wires are on the side," I replied.

"That won't work. First you have to change the bales so the cut and folded edges are on the sides, not top and bottom."

In one little sentence Cedar Rose gave me two bigger-than-I-could-swallow bites to chew on. Through the years, how many thousands of little "square" (they were actually rectangular) bales had I lifted and thrown and stacked? And had I ever noticed that one edge was folded, the opposite cut?

When I thought about how a baler worked it made perfect sense. It raked hay into its five-foot mouth, plunging the wad to the back of its throat every few seconds. At the end of each stroke, a knife cut the hay on the open side to square up the bale. After a certain amount was stuffed down its throat, two needles stabbed through the wad of hay, their twine (or wire) lines caught by the knotters and magically spun 360 degrees to make a loop. And then, more magically, the ends were cut and pulled through the loop to tie the knot. The whole knotting process was complete in the blink of an eye.

My old International Harvester baler manual had a whole page of photos in the troubleshooting section dedicated to incorrectly tied knots. I think I'd seen every example in real life. Never having run a wire-tied baler, I can only imagine from a safe distance the full implications of the phrase, "everything went haywire!"

The resulting bale was pushed out the back end of the machine to rest with its strings (or wires) upon the ground. Back when I was fifteen and working on a hay crew for Gib Griffin, if I'd realized that one side of the bale had cut edges and the other had folded edges, I could have saved myself a few ruined long sleeved shirts and scratched forearms by always picking up on the folded side.

That thought digested, I couldn't begin to face the bigger bite that Cedar Rose was offering.

"The tops and bottoms of the bales are slick and won't hold mud or plaster. The cut and folded edges are like straw ends. If you want to get away from metal lathe, you must have the cut and folded edges showing."

"Well, that's not an option," I replied flatly. "We've already got half the bales in."

Cedar Rose's silence offered no compromise.

---

**Green House Journal**
**October 14, 1998**

*100+ straw bales in! Windows in. Roof done.*

---

**October 19, 1998**

*Straw bales must be turned flat to accept earthen plaster! Felt underneath is rather toxic. Sooo…we'll switch bales and put cedar 2 x 6s under…*

---

It took about two days of solid chewing but we finally swallowed the bitter pill and decided to do as Cedar Rose suggested and take out all those bales we put in with Ken and Andy.

The problem wasn't just doing the work over. Straw bales were pretty easy to move around. It took only one day for the four of us to set those hundred bales. No, the real problem was that when placed with the wires up, the bales would be eighteen inches wide, about three inches wider than when their wires are on the side, the way we first had them. So our house interior space was just about to shrink by three inches on all sides. Since we had already framed in all the interior walls (eight of them reached to the edge of the house), we now had to cut three inches off the ends of all interior walls to accommodate the wider bales.

Cedar Rose also told us to scrap the tar paper we had placed under the bottom row of bales to keep them from wicking up moisture from the cement. "Tar paper is petroleum based and off-gases toxic chemicals," she warned.

She recommended a complex, expensive, and very Zen-looking solution for keeping the bales high and dry. Once we had removed all the bales and pulled off all the brand new but toxin-breathing tar paper and were looking at our bare concrete slab again, we painted the outside eighteen inches of the slab with a black, non-toxic sealer. On the edges of that we nailed down a pair of cedar two-by-sixes, six inches apart.

Our architect/designer friend, Chelle, helping out that day, shoveled pea gravel between the cedar runners while I nailed the boards into the cement ahead of her and Alice hoisted the first row of bales over the rebar skewers behind her.

"It looks like something out of a Japanese garden!" Chelle laughed.

"Oommm..." I jokingly meditated between the obnoxious bangs of my .22 caliber nail driver.

Should any moisture get on the slab now, it will still be two inches from the bottom of our bales. I think if I were building another straw bale home, I'd pour an extra two inches of concrete on the foundation and do away with the pea-gravel boardwalk despite its soul-calming appearance and lovely cedar smell.

Not only that, I'd pour the whole footing differently because of what we had to do when we finally decided on the material for our exterior walls.

# CHAPTER 6
## ...AND STONE

WE SAT IN our lawn chairs on our break considering the options for the twentieth time. Okay, we could plaster the walls like Jerry did but without the metal lathe. But would it hold and did we really want cement walls? How long would they last and would we have to paint them?

We could use an earthen mud like our friend Lonnie Gamble in Fairfield, Iowa had used on his straw bale home. Lonnie even showed us how to mix it up and apply it. We liked the very natural look and feel. The trouble with mud, we thought, was that we needed large overhangs to protect it from our frequent driving rains. But large overhangs cut out winter sunlight that warmed the house for free. If the walls eroded we would have a yearly chore of mixing up mud and patching. That definitely failed the "no maintenance" test.

We considered a hybrid wall of mud above and something less erosive below where most of the rain would hit. But what could we put below? Cedar siding was natural, smelled nice – at least at first, but required a preservative application every few years.

What we were really searching for was a natural material that looked nice and required no maintenance whatsoever. So far we were coming up empty-handed, but there was no huge hurry. After we had put all the straw bales in, laying them flat with the wires up, we covered the whole house with plastic to keep the rain and snow off.

---

### Green House Journal
### January 26, 1999

*Happy New Year! Bales all in and very nice. Much more dense and secure feeling...*

---

With the house "walled in" and covered with plastic, our attention focused on the interior. But winter passed, spring came and we were no closer to solving the outside wall problem.

At least we were driving in to our house now instead of the quarter mile walk carrying tools from Norman's house. There were no good access roads. The road along Gees Creek on our southern border was dirt in the summer but deep mud in the winter and spring.

When we poured the cement foundation with Jerry and his crew, we had to give the cement truck driver directions to Norman's house, then beyond into a pasture, east through two gates then south until he saw the construction site. It was a bit unusual.

We rejoiced when we finally heard the first truck lumbering through the pasture.

"You found us!" we called up to him.

"I thought for sure somebody was playing a joke on me!" he yelled back from the cab.

The rest of the trucks followed his tracks through the grass.

Since our old farm was adjacent to a quarry, Alice and I picked up a $10 load of gravel every day on our way to the property and ladled it out on our vertical driveway. Soon we had it tamed to where a two-wheel drive vehicle could get up. Providing it was dry.

The graveling of our road was another minor miracle.

A Jamesport couple, seeking a "hideout" like us, bought a small bramble patch strewn with rusted machinery a quarter mile from us. Gary and Carol Ellis owned the premiere antique store in Jamesport, had lived in an apartment above it, and were responsible, in great part, for putting Jamesport on the map as a tourist destination. Both of them have an incredible eye for art and design and saw the potential paradise in the diamond-in-the-rough bramble patch.

Their house site bordered Poosey Conservation Area and was barely in sight of Menno Graber's place. Gary and Carol paid for a quarter mile of gravel out of their own pockets and we were the beneficiaries. We had always figured we'd have to pay for almost ¾ of a mile of gravel to fix up the road leading to our steep driveway but Gary and Carol beat us to the punch on the first leg.

But the next thing we knew, the township was graveling from Gary and Carol's to our driveway! Turns out that little mud trail was a county road! Still, I'm not certain we would ever have got help with the gravel if it hadn't been for Richard.

Richard Morris grew up on our farm and owned the land adjacent to us on the opposite side from Gary and Carol. Without any lobbying from us, Richard organized the graveling and opening up of our dirt road. We were very lucky to have the best road grater operator in the county do the work, too: Richard!

Richard and all the neighbors pitched in to trim overhanging trees and widen the road enough to allow a gravel truck through and help pay for the first load of gravel. Norman was down in our valley with a chain saw before anyone else.

The beautiful new bed of gravel that appeared on our road one day was like a fresh fallen snow. No more walks in. We had a beautiful, curving, driveway through the prettiest drive in the county.

Yet, there was just a pinch of remorse over opening up this road. We were attuned to the wildlife and knew what it meant to some of them. We haven't seen bobcat tracks since we put in the road. I wondered if many pioneers felt regret over opening new trails through pristine areas.

Not long after the road opened, the Ellises began work on their corner of paradise. Theirs went up much faster since they had a full time crew working on it. It was fun for us to watch the development even though it was obvious they were going to pass us by quickly.

Sure enough, one day we drove by and they were already putting stone on their walls. Stone on the walls! We drove in and took a look. Gary had collected field limestone and other weird and interesting rocks and Johnny Kurtz and a crew of young Amish men were laying it up like bricks. It had a very nice look to it and they seemed to be having fun because it was so unusual.

We spoke with Johnny. His estimate on Gary and Carol Ellis's work was $16,000. Our house was only slightly smaller and would probably cost $14,000. Our hearts sank because it was way over our budget. In addition, Johnny couldn't get to it for four months.

Oh well, we enjoyed watching them put the rocks on and thought more about stones ourselves. We had access to plenty. The old farm had a root cellar and foundation at the old Romesburg place. Plus we had lots of stone on the hills and creeks of the new farm.

Stone just seemed perfect except for the cost and timing. It was free if we picked it up and cleaned it and stacked it near the masonry crew. It required no maintenance. It blended well in nature. And it provided a very strong exterior.

Not lost on us was the completion of the three little pigs story since we already had straw and "sticks" (our mill-cut timbers) in the house. By this time we had had hundreds of visitors drive by even though we were on the way to nowhere. We had heard the three little pigs joke so many times now that we had to pretend it was still funny whenever someone said it.

Of course, fate or luck, or whatever you want to call it, went our way as always. Johnny's very efficient crew finished up in half the time they expected. Because they were used to laying small bricks and the Ellis's was their first stone house, they overestimated the time by double! Yes, our new estimate was $7000!

Johnny said, "Could you get the rock out there in two weeks? We just had an opening."

"Two weeks? Yes! We'll get the rock out there!"

Everything else went on hold and we madly gathered up stones, once again amazed at how things always worked out for us.

# CHAPTER 7
# HORSE SENSE

*If one advances confidently in the direction of his dreams, and
endeavors to live the life which he has imagined, he will meet with
a success unexpected in common hours.*

HENRY DAVID THOREAU, Walden

STONE WALLS ARE heavy. And they don't just stick like Velcro to straw
bales. Johnny had never done anything like this before – the Ellis's was
his first stone work - and, as far as we know, no straw bale home besides
ours has stone walls. The marriage of straw and stone required a few major
modifications.

First we had to dig a footing to support the weight of the stone wall.
Well, I managed to get out of that job. Fortunately, Johnny and his son,
David, and the two others on the crew, Raymond Mast and William Ray
Detweiler, were willing to dig the three foot deep trench around the two
hundred foot circumference of our house.

Alice and I had to add a framework of 2 x 4s all around the house to attach
the wall holders to. Wall holders are corrugated strips of metal used by
masons to "tie" the bricks to the wood frame. They nail one end into the
wood frame, and then bend the metal in a right angle so that it sits in
plaster in a seam between two bricks. A wall holder every two or three feet
is enough to tie the bricks – or stones – to the house frame.

Since our straw bale house "framework" only existed around the doors
and windows, we had to cut slots in the hay and insert 2 x 4s, tying them
to the cedar 2 x 6 on the concrete and the header at the top. This and the
trench after-thought is probably where William Ray got his first notion of

us making things hard on ourselves. But we were delighted to do the extra work if the stone walls were going to turn out like we thought they were.

After that, all Alice and I had to do was collect rock. Pry out rock. Wash rock. Unload rock. And stack rock. Our good friends Tad and Ann Trombley made the grave mistake of helping us on a rock-collecting day. After collecting and emptying two pick-up loads I was pleasantly exhausted and ready for shade and a cool drink.

"Shall we get one more load?" Alice asked the group, her voice fresh and chipper.

Before I could groan, Tad – a world class athlete who recently won the national 100-meter competition in his age bracket - said, "Why not?"

I couldn't very well answer that question the way I wanted to. Free labor was not to be argued with. I'm pretty sure Ann and I could have made a case for moderation, but we continued to haul rock like prisoners through the heat of the afternoon.

Johnny and his boys wasted no time trenching. We poured the cement footing, let it cure and they began laying up the stones during one of the hottest stretches in a July we've ever seen. They emptied their thermoses in the early afternoon and we replenished their water. But boy could they put up the rock!

And the bigger the stones the better as far as the boys were concerned. As a team, they hauled several hundred-pounders up in to place, plastered them in and wedged a two-by-four against the ground while they set up. I looked long and hard at that operation but I couldn't fault the engineering. As long as they rested on a solid foundation and didn't lean out, those giants were going to stick and offered fewer seams to plaster. Which was the key attraction to the crew.

Two times Johnny said with his trademark smile, "It looks like we'll be needing some more rock soon, David."

We placed pallets of layered stones all around the house and they'd haul individual stones up on to their scaffolding and choose the right one for the spot. They weren't too interested in using smaller stones, but they also culled for thickness and irregularity. We wound up with a healthy pile of rejects and had to scramble for more good rock.

Sometimes they'd have to hammer a little off a stone to make it fit right. Johnny's crew looked like they'd been working field stone all their lives. Especially Johnny. Johnny was the most efficient worker we'd ever seen. Not a motion was wasted.

"You ought to see him tape sheet rock," Mary Kauffman remarked after we told her how fast Johnny could work.

A few months later we got the chance. We asked Johnny if he'd help us finish mudding and taping the sheet rock. There were only a few jobs on the house Alice and I didn't do by ourselves: pour cement, put the stones up, and the solar power installation. We had done plenty of taping and mudding before and we weren't especially talented or fast at it, so, remembering that Johnny – who was a whiz at something he'd never done before – was sort of famous for his sheet rock taping, we splurged a little and asked if he'd help.

It wasn't a splurge at all. Probably the best money we spent. Mudding and taping is where you hide the seams of the sheet rock or dry wall before painting. It needs to be neat. Invisibility is the goal.

I took note of Johnny's unusual gear: stilts, ironing board (well, that's what it looked like), old milk jug and a few trowels. He mixed up half a milk jug of plaster and set it on his ironing board. I noticed the jug had a narrow slit in it about half way up. Then he took a roll of sheetrock tape and put it on a roller - just like a roll of toilet paper – attached to his ironing board. This was going to be a good show!

He strapped his stilts on, hoisted himself up and threaded the paper roll through the slit in the milk jug. Slick! Then he pulled out an arm's length of tape neatly smeared with plaster. Then he pulled out another arm's length and made a loop. Then he pulled another and another and another until he had enough mudded tape in one long, looped line to span the entire living room ceiling. With a twist he tore the tape and stilted over to the edge of the wall.

This was the best part. He stuck the end of the tape at the joint against the wall, took several backwards steps (yep, still on stilts) and, with a flick, stuck the tape on the ceiling directly over the seam! Two steps back, flick. Two steps back, flick. In 15 seconds the tape was all up! Then he walked forward and smoothed it all in one pass with his trowel. How he'd learned to do this, I can't imagine, but I'd bet money on Johnny in a mudding contest with anybody.

Cousin Paul was visiting about that time and we had begun the mudding marathon on the inside of the house. He asked if he could use the stilts. We didn't think Johnny would mind so he put them on and we helped him up. He seemed pretty stable and was doing fine until Alice asked him a question and he looked over his shoulder to answer.

The movement threw his balance off enough that he began to lean backwards.

"Oh no," he understated, committed to a slow crash landing.

His slow motion fall was probably worse than the landing on his butt. His wife Lynn rushed to his side but the biggest bruises were on his pride. He took the stilts off, still chuckling.

Johnny's legendary talent (we'd been bragging about him, of course) just raised a notch in everyone's estimation. He had mastered what it took to do that job in the most efficient way possible. I imagined Johnny was just as practical in everything he undertook.

Their practicality is one of the many things we admire about our new Amish neighbors. Their lives are more deeply rooted in the physical world of soil and livestock, garden and horse-and-buggy, and that yields a higher level of common sense - that commodity that "ain't so common anymore" as Missouri's own farmer advocate and social commentator, Derry Brownfield, notes in his regular radio program – the Common Sense Coalition.

Common sense is born of solving problems with the mind and hands. I came from a lineage that used both hand and mind but heavily favored the mind side. I was clumsy and impatient with tools when I first started using them. Finding a proper rhythm with physical work was a joy that I discovered much later.

My Dad, Paul Evans Schafer, worked in the cerebral world of calculations and designs and drafting plans for sewage systems, water retaining dams and water purification plants. His Dad, Paul Abbot Schafer, studied and taught geology and the art and science of extracting minerals from the earth. And his Dad, Joseph Schafer, was an academician consumed with books and the study of American pioneer history.

Each of them had their connection back to the land. My Dad spent a lot of time on site studying the land before construction projects and overseeing implementation of plans during construction. Grandpa walked over thousands of miles of land and observed it like few people have the chance to do. My great grandfather, Joseph, had such a fascination for history that he rode a bicycle the length of the Oregon Trail.

But for the most part, the careers of civil engineers, geologists and historians are spent at the desk thinking, studying, drafting and writing. This was the track I was on, too, studying biology at college. I liked to use my mind; that was my paternal history for three generations and I never gave farming as a career a thought until my Dad suggested it as an option.

At first I was offended. It seemed a giant step backward; a waste of any mental talent I might have. The trouble is, I have to go back to my great, great grandfather, Joseph's father, Matthias, to find a farmer in the family. I had no family role models, only stories.

Matthias was actually quite a guy. As a younger son, he knew he was not in line to run the family vineyards on the north bank of the beautiful Mosel River across from Bernkastel, Germany. He was a sharp student and went all the way to Trier to school – they called it gymnasium – and had Karl Marx as a classmate. Whether true or not, family folklore has it that Karl won the award for literature in gymnasium and Matthias won it in math.

The only other story remaining from that era was that Matthias was in gymnasium when the news of the death of the great German thinker and author, Goethe, interrupted classes. Marx discussed Goethe's life work with his teachers while the other boys played games.

Matthias immigrated to Grant County, Wisconsin, raised fourteen children spanning two wives and despised the communist writing of his former classmate, Carl Marx. Matthias farmed his rich land and served as the town scribe of Muscoda. He left us a lovely piece of writing called, simply, "Neighbors," in which he tells of every farmer bordering him, their ethnic background, idiosyncrasies, farming practices and selected anecdotes.

Although Matthias would have been the perfect role model for me – the farmer who also loved literature and writing, I didn't learn about him until I had already chosen the rural life. My spirit thrives in the outdoors and working with my hands. That balancing and grounding influence in my life would be difficult to find in an urban environment.

The Amish are more like Matthias than I am. From a very young age, they help in the gardens, ride horses, milk cows and butcher chickens. At night, without television or radio, they read, visit, play games, do bookwork and write letters. Most of the Amish kids I know love to read and do a lot of it.

I had a care-free childhood, growing up in friendly Kansas City and finishing school in Manila, Philippines and San Juan, Puerto Rico. After four years in a demanding college I was turned loose on the world with the official American stamp of approval – a college diploma. I didn't realize until I'd farmed a little while that I was embarrassingly deficient in a commodity that was essential to farming and important in life as well: horse sense.

Horse sense, practicality, common sense, good judgment, call it what you will. I value it because I came about it the hard way. I could see that growing up Amish almost guarantees a healthy measure of horse sense. Then there are a few exceptional people like Johnny Kurtz who take practicality to it's highest level, like an art form.

This giant switch in lifestyle – from 540-acre farm to 64-acre farm, from 80 momma cows to zero momma cows, from year-round livestock to three-season livestock, and from inefficient, old farmhouse to new, alternative home – represents a commitment to simplicity and practicality. Paring down to the essentials in life is like peeling the layers of onion skin away to find the core of ourselves.

And, yes, the onion skin metaphor is complete with tears. As we shed the superficial layers we expose more of ourselves and have to deal honestly with who we are. I am so lucky – though I've cursed it a thousand times – to have a mate who will not tolerate the slightest misunderstanding. With dear Alice, there are no forbidden topics, no grey areas of communication left to fester, no issues set aside because they seem prickly, touchy, or unsolvable.

With no children to split our attention and Alice's unwavering dedication to keep us in tune with each other, our relationship became a toboggan ride of self discovery culminating in crafting a living and working environment in which we can thrive. It is a thrilling adventure and the Amish play a very big part in it, not only as role models of simple, practical living, but as resources, friends and mirrors to help us see ourselves more clearly.

We are not consciously trying to live as simply as the Amish. We are just trying to live exactly as we want and that means paring down a lot, getting rid of a lot of excessive chores and making life easier.

"Simple down, son," my Jamesport buddy, Jim Woodward, puts it. "We've got to simple down."

To many, the simplicity of the Amish seems like suffering and self-denial. No electricity. How hard would that be for the rest of us? Can you imagine life without lights at the flick of a switch? Alice and I are used to no dish washers or clothes dryers now, but how about pins instead of buttons on Alice's clothes? Her fingers would be covered in band-aids!

And speaking of clothes, how about making clothes for all the family? And – speaking of family – how about no birth control? Fourteen children like Matthias is a lot but every Amish is related to a family that big or bigger!

When I focus on all the things they do without it seems like such a difficult life they lead. And that's what made William Ray's comment so ironic.

I never got to know William Ray Detweiler well enough to really break the ice. We picked him up with the rest of the masonry crew, chatted a little on the drives and they worked hard. It's my experience that most of the Amish are a little standoffish with us "English" until you've spent enough time together to break the ice.

Once the ice is broken, they shine from within. The deceptions and game-playing of modern society are virtually non-existent among the Amish. They feel good about themselves and when they smile and laugh it is without hesitation or reservation.

William Ray stood back at a safe distance watching me weed-wipe the straw bale walls. Wheat-straw dust billowed out of the room and covered me from head to toe. I was trimming up the scraggly edges - sort of a wall hair cut - prior to applying the first mud plaster.

Alice and I had dealt with a certain amount of embarrassment over this house. Sure, the three little pigs joke was a good yuck, but there was also some incredulity involved, too. For the eight months the straw walls were bare and a parade of visitors saw them, we saw the insanity of the house through their eyes. It looked like a barn.

"What about mice?" was usually the second question after, "What about fire?"

Fire was easy. There's so little air in a tight bale they don't burn, they just smolder. It takes four hours to burn through a straw bale wall compared to 15 minutes to burn through a typical frame wall.

The question of mice was trickier. We shirked it easily saying, "Oh the walls will be covered and they won't get in."

We never mentioned that the straw bales were full of wheat and we had ourselves a real mouse vacation resort for quite some time.

The most horrific event – I can tell it now that, thank God, no one ever found out about it – I can blame on Cedar Rose. She went too far that time.

"Can you get cow manure?" Cedar Rose asked us when we were finally ready to plaster the walls.

Can we get cow manure? We considered ourselves cow manure experts, authorities, and connoisseurs! We had made a study of judging the nutritional intake of livestock by assessing their nutritional output, that is, their poop.

If the poop is stacked up high, the diet is too fibrous to gain much, if any, weight. If the poop is watery, there is too little fiber and the nutrients pass through too quickly to be absorbed. There was every gradation of poop firmness in between, but the ideal bovine poop (and we made planning decisions based on this, really!) has the firmness of a pumpkin pie. It's spread out and an inch or two thick when it drops and holds a peak like whipped cream in the center. That's two to three pound-per-day-gain poop. Good stuff.

"Why do we want manure?"

"Manure has proteins that make the best binding material with mud."

This wasn't a witch doctor formula. Cedar Rose had studied earth home construction in France. Maybe in some cafe a couple of Frenchmen right this minute are laughing their berets off and spewing their Burgundy over the naïve American girl slopping cow crap on houses, I don't know.

It didn't take long for us to realize it was a bad joke. Very bad.

Maybe our high octane, three-pound-a-day poop, had an extra offensive odor that Cedar Rose's Rocky Mountain cow poop didn't. Whatever the case, we knew we'd made a huge mistake as soon as we'd spread it around a few window frames.

"It makes the best first layer," she said. "The following mud coat will bind strongly to it."

47

Right. All we knew is that the stench would gag a maggot. We opened all the windows and doors and put a hex on the driveway to keep visitors away. Thank God none showed up. We could imagine how much fun our new neighbors would have with that!

A straw bale house was cute and weird. But smearing cow dung on the walls? Foul! Kinky! Satanic! We'd never last in Jamesport if that got out.

I finally stopped the weed wiping frenzy, stepped back out of the room to let the dust settle and noticed William Ray studying me from a safe distance.

"What are you doing?" he finally asked as I struggled to pull off my hat, fogged-up safety goggles, and tangled respirator.

"Giving the straw bales a haircut!" I grinned hoping he'd find humor in spite of the ridiculousness. It didn't sell.

He thought for a while, and then delivered the knockout punch before turning and walking away.

"You sure do make things hard on yourself!"

I stood there watching William Ray walk away and nodding my head in agreement. A buggy-driving, electricity-shunning fellow thought I made things hard on myself...

But I found the common thread between us and it was immediately satisfying. A life of simplicity doesn't just happen by doing nothing; that creates chaos. Crafting a framework for simple living takes discipline, determination and, yes, a very occasional episode of "making things hard on yourself."

# CHAPTER 8
# ON THE WALLS – MUD!

THE STONE WALLS Johnny Kurtz and his crew put up turned out to be everything we wanted. They required no maintenance, they looked great, and even though it seemed like a lot of money to us, friends from the city said exterior stone walls cost many times more than what we paid – especially if you buy the rock. We were so grateful for the talented Amish crew and Gary and Carol who did the stone experimenting right next door.

But when it came to the interior walls, we were on our own. All along we planned to use natural mud plaster using the local clay that north Missouri is famous for. We saved a huge pile of it from our cistern excavation. Cedar Rose said we could do it. Lonnie Gamble said we could do it. I guess it wasn't a complete leap of faith. It just felt like it.

We carefully separated topsoil from subsoil during the cistern excavation. Under our one large (30 x 90') shed, neighbor Elvan Schrock and his son Vernon, poured us two water storage rooms – each eight foot square and holding 3000 gallons of water. Sharing a wall with them was a smaller root cellar. Our shed floor made their ceilings and extended beyond.

We like the idea of sharing walls and getting more mileage out of the cement. The shop floor was, therefore, a dual purpose structure – both floor and ceiling. The cisterns and root cellar shared a wall. The stairs to the root cellar in the middle of the shop floor made a perfect pit to change oil in the vehicles. The shed itself not only protected our vehicles and shop but also collected 1000 gallons of water with every inch of rain.

The notion of dual purpose structures is a sound design principle – one of the tenets of a discipline called permaculture - and one we tried to apply as often as possible. The inside walls of the house fell into the dual purpose category, too. We hoped the ample thickness and soft curves would not only provide great insulation, but also a pleasing feeling of warmth and protection as well as a visual delight.

We felt that way in many of the adobe houses we visited in New Mexico. The difference between adobe and straw bale houses was only that adobe was solid clay. Many New Mexican builders were going to straw bale construction to achieve the same look at a lower price.

After our excavation clay dried, I scooped up bucketfuls with our tractor front loader and sifted them through a screen over a large, empty stock watering tank. This yielded sand grain-sized clay particles. It was a slow process. When the tank was pretty full, we shoveled the fine clay into feed sacks and squirreled them away like walnuts for winter.

We would need some ultra-fine blend and some coarse blend for this project. Cedar Rose had recipes for every layer. The idea was to graduate from straw-binding mud which had to be really thin – the pancake batter stuff – to mud that stood up and worked just like cement.

We carefully wheelbarrowed the first load of "pancake batter" into the house. It looked like a witch's brew, too thick to drink and too thin to put on a trowel.

"How are we going to apply this stuff?" I said.

More questions and doubts chased each other silently in my tormented mind. "This is the moment of decision. Do we REALLY want to smear mud on our house?" Mud huts were not an uplifting image right now.

"Is this REALLY going to work?" Again, the Cedar Rose doubts. We had replaced over 100 straw bales just to turn them sideways. We had ripped out brand new tarpaper. We had installed expensive water protection under the bales. We had shortened all the interior walls by three inches, decreasing our living space as we did it. Finally, we had placed all the straw bales flat, meaning we had to use 20 – 30% more bales in the long run.

And why had we done all of that? Just so the mud would stick without using metal lathe!

Was I nuts? Jerry Tichener wouldn't hesitate to say yes, I knew that much. Plenty of practical folks – just like William Ray Detweiler – would probably agree. In a few seconds doubts had swarmed over me like angry bees. I was paralyzed, both mentally and physically.

Alice, responding to the only thing I'd actually said aloud, replied, "We'll put it on with our hands!"

She pushed the wheelbarrow right into the straw, dipped her cupped hands into the brew and slathered in on the walls without a second's hesitation. I was aghast. It was an abomination! As obscene as graffiti. Wrong, wrong, wrong!

"Come on!" Alice cried out. "It's fun!"

In no time she had splotched a large section of wall and was squealing with delight as the mud dripped off her elbows.

Like a zombie, I approached the wheel barrow and plunged my hands into the snake pit of venomous goo. But instead of venom and snakes I felt caressing warmth and wetness.

The spell broke instantly. I was baptized in the mud. My doubts and fears vanished as the child within was reborn! I found my faith again.

Faith was a good thing. We were going to need a lot of it.

There were four, separate mud coat applications. First, the pancake batter slip-coat making the straw bales look like cocoanut bars dipped in chocolate. Then, a thicker, dryer coat with small bits of straw mixed in. This batch wasn't spread over the walls; it filled the seams between bales and shaped corners and odd spots.

Oh yes, there were odd spots. Straw bales don't just go up like tinker toys to make a flush wall. There were lots of variations. The wall-straightening tool of choice is a spade. You wind up and swing it like a baseball bat into the sides to shape them.

I wonder if William Ray saw me whacking the walls with a spade. He probably thought I'd lost my mind with frustration over the whole thing. I'm glad no one saw our technique for preparing the small bits of hay for that fill coat.

Using the same old stock water tank that we'd used to filter the clay, we flaked off and fluffed up a little straw on one side. Then we lifted our push mower into the tank, yanked the start cord and mowed the straw into shreds.

We should have made a movie titled, "What is he doing?" The film would begin showing a normal-looking shed with a truck and tractor parked underneath, bird song in the background. Then a pan left to show two big sliding doors opened. Zoom in to reveal a grinning mad man standing inside a water tank. His hands are holding the handle bars of a mysterious implement submerged in the tank.

As if preparing to fly off, the madman waves and lowers his goggles, still grinning. He pulls a cord and an incredible racket vibrates out of the stock tank and through the shed. He gives one last insane look at the camera and points to his ears. A close zoom shows ear plugs so the kids who try this at home remember to think, "safety first."

Zoom out. The grin fades into high dive-serious contemplation. The handle bars are pushed down, then forward, then slowly released up and an instant tornado of straw engulfs the mad man as he dances wildly back and forth inside the tank.

Well, how would you have done it?

The seam-filling "coat" with the chopped straw was more like mud balls and mud baguettes than a "coat." But, for credit, I'm counting it as a coat. It was a separate step. Every bale required several balls and baguettes. And even though it didn't drip down our arms and we didn't use a trowel, it's only fair to count it as another layer of mud.

The third coat had more sand in it and less straw. With the seams plugged and the third coat applied, the walls began to show their personality. We tried to even up the remaining dips and valleys with this coat.

The fourth coat used the finest clay, some sand and only a little straw.

In each of these coats, by the way, was a flour paste to help bind the mud. This is not your standard first-grade paper Mache mix. Oh no. This paste came from a secret French recipe developed under the watchful eye of Charlemagne and was handed down through the centuries, like maps to the secret treasure chambers of the Knights Templar. The recipe was thought to be lost for most of the last century. Fortunately, and through heroic efforts, Cedar Rose had found the ancient formula and escaped with it to America.

Well, sometimes it seemed that dramatic. Cooking up this paste was a very elaborate procedure, bordering on a chemistry class experiment. I worried about the walls sagging like Dali clocks if we had the temperature a degree or two off or if the cooking time was a little short or long.

Then I'd go to the other extreme. "These walls are going to last for centuries whether we add this silly flour paste to the mud or not!"

My fantasy mind took me back to those French conspirators who certainly snookered innocent Cedar Rose. Again I imagined them snorting Burgundy through their handle-bar moustaches as they thought of us Yanks actually cooking flour and water and mixing the brew into mud and making houses out of it.

We country folk can be pretty naïve, you know.

A friend of mine, whom I'll not embarrass by naming, once mentioned in an offhand way that he thought the White Park breed of cattle had white meat.

"Where did you get that idea?" I asked.

"A fellow told me so."

"Did you believe him?"

"Well, I didn't have any reason not to."

Innocent until proven guilty is a noble philosophy and this gentleman lived by the Golden Rule. Since he would never deceive someone else, why would someone do that to him?

In this diverse world, there are a few scoundrels along with the vast majority of upstanding citizens, and, maybe it takes one to know one, but somewhere along the line I'd encountered a few rascals and lost a good percentage of my naïveté. For better or worse, that's the way it is. Maybe I unfairly doubted Cedar Rose's recipes, but I was absolutely positive White Park cattle had red meat inside them.

(Cedar Rose's infamous manure concoction later proved itself after we left it out of the recipe on a few window sills and found that the manure-free mud paste dried and cracked and fell off. We collected more manure, did the job over, held our noses, opened the windows and cast hexes and spells to keep gossiping visitors away.)

The flour paste spooked us a little at first, too, but before too long, we decided it was going to stick and we stuck with the formula. This final coat was the money coat, the coat we – and everyone else – would be looking at forever and ever, Amen. We got fussy with this coat, despite the fact that by this layer we were walking around with our knuckles dragging on the ground our arms were so heavy from troweling, troweling, troweling.

But no matter how fussy we were, there were still many ripples and ridges, globs and trowel lines. When we carefully erased one line, we made three more! We were not professional plasterers and all our muscles from the wrist up to the brain were dead against the idea of prolonging the agony. That made the next big crossroads a mind-over-body contest.

In typical fashion, we arrived at the "end" of the mudding before finalizing the next step. In fairness, we originally thought there would be no next step. We would have beautiful, smooth, mud plastered, natural walls on the inside and that was the end of it.

But there were two problems. First, how were we going to blend the interior walls – which were not straw bale – with the exterior mud-covered walls?

Second, the mud wasn't as light colored as we anticipated, making our already small rooms look smaller and dark.

Okay, no problem. We would just have to paint the walls.

We looked into natural paints because natural paints are porous and straw bale walls must breathe. They can't be sealed tight or moisture will become trapped inside and the straw will soon look like shredded wheat left in the milk until lunch. Then it will slowly melt into a gooey, stinky, moldy mass at the base of the hollow walls and – well, the thought is so hideous, I don't want to explore it further. Straw bale walls must breathe.

Natural paints, unlike latex and oil-based, are made of a milk base and do not completely seal the surface they cover. They are expensive, but, well, we'd bite the bullet on this one.

Then we realized that no natural paint was going to cover our dark brown walls. We needed a white base first. Okay, a white base coat. We could live with that; we'd just put two coats on.

Well, we thought that through and the idea collapsed. Natural paint is thin and wouldn't really cover the dark walls. Then we had the brilliant idea: Why not put sheet rock mud over the clay mud? Not only would that give us a suitable surface for the natural paint, but we could then blend in with the interior walls.

But – oh dear! – that meant troweling mud over the entire surface of the house one more time! We could barely stand the thought and had to keep it a close secret from our arms and shoulders until the final hour.

But it did give us one more chance to get the very last of those nasty little ridges and imperfections out of our increasingly gorgeous walls. Yes, the whiteness was purifying, elevating, expanding. We watched the house change like an arctic hare into its winter white.

Our muscles warmed up and loosened up and, old pros that we were, we slicked up those walls even more. But still, there were ridges left behind. Oh well. Once we painted, it would be gorgeous.

We began looking more deeply into the natural paints as we neared the second end of all the plastering. It was hard finding a color we liked and, my! but these paints were expensive. And not that easy to clean either, we were learning a little too late.

"I wonder how often we'll have to re-paint the walls," I said aloud, letting the unspoken violation of the "little to no maintenance" code hang in the air like a bad odor.

It was such a stumper we just had to back away from it for a while.

Then I got the brilliant idea to do what any sensible teenager would have done at the very first consideration of the problem. I surfed the internet.

Immediately I found a gorgeous straw bale home in Colorado with walls that looked like parchment, a buttery, mottled, yellow that was soft yet bright. Best of all, it was nothing more than sheet rock mud mixed with ferrous sulfate – an inexpensive fertilizer and all we had to do was mix it up and plaster it on.

Yes, there it was staring us in the face: One…More…Coat.

The relief we felt that knowing it would definitely, without question, be the final coat, it would look great, be maintenance free, blend with the interior walls, AND brighten the house almost made the undertaking bearable.

We bought another box car load of sheet rock mud and ordered the micronutrient. Maybe this time the ridges would come out. We really didn't care.

We mixed the ferrous sulfate to the exact proportions told us by the nice home owner in Colorado: Mix about half a Dixie cup of ferrous sulfate powder to about a quart of water and then mix about a ¼ cup of that in a five gallon bucket of sheet rock mud. This was chemistry more at our level of precision.

I attached a mixing tool to our strong drill and mixed the brew with anticipation. Alice expertly troweled a big dollop onto the mud plate in her left hand and went to the little battery room where we always started. It would be the least seen room so our technique could improve from there and, God forbid, if there was some disaster we wouldn't have to see it as often.

"It's GREEN!" Alice shrieked.

"What?"

"It turned green! Come here. Are you sure you mixed it right?"

"Yes, I think so," I said, not at all sure.

"And you ordered the right stuff?" Alice was in full Spanish Inquisition mode now and I was starting to break a sweat.

"Just what the woman in Colorado told me."

Oh, did that sound lame. What woman? She doesn't even have a name? Does she know ferrous sulfate from carrot bunt cake? She probably flunked chemistry. Or maybe she was friends of the French guys! Hey! Colorado... Cedar Rose...? No! No way. The paranoids were definitely after me. I had to round up my stampeding thoughts.

We both stared incredulously at the hideous slime green plaster, our hearts breaking. And then a miracle happened. Well, it was actually just oxygen reacting with the ferrous sulfate, but it was like a miracle to us. The slime green turned, slowly but surely, into a beautiful buttery yellow. It was gorgeous. We danced a jig and plastered beyond sunset.

# Chapter 9
# Off the Walls: Henry Schrock's Cabinets

THE FINAL LAYER of beautiful, buttery plaster was a joy to put on. It was almost as if we waved a magic wand over the walls whenever our trowels slathered on the mix. In no time our house took on a whole new serene and beautiful personality.

What a metamorphosis! From the unruly larvae of a scruffy barn loft to a primitive mud-hut caterpillar, it then emerged to this lovely butterfly with a graceful adobe look.

The inside of the house came together in a blizzard of activity. Henry Schrock had been building our oak cabinets for quite some time. We had contracted with him over a year earlier just to get on his busy schedule. Henry's work was well known in the area and beyond despite the fact that he was still a young man. His craftsmanship was excellent.

Henry was absolutely straightforward without a hint of salesman in him, but he couldn't have hooked us more solidly when we first visited his shop. The layout was impressive with machines nicely spaced and handy. A gang shaft to run them lay buried in a trough in the cement floor. The rotating shaft was safely covered with wood. A large diesel engine in a separate room powered the gang shaft.

Overhead and on several walls were pipes with fittings for air hoses. The engine also ran a compressor that filled large air tanks. With pulley and air power, Henry's shop could do anything an electric cabinet shop could do.

It was neat as a pin. Vacuum hoses pulled in sawdust and shavings from various stations and deposited them into large containers. All hand tools had their place. Henry was obviously well organized.

What hooked us, though, was not so much his impressive shop but what we found next door. In the large, adjoining room, away from the sawdust, Henry varnished the completed cabinets, dressers, tables, and other items he had custom made. You could say it was his show room.

Alice and I were immediately drawn to the beautiful oak table. In our eighteen years of farm life, our eating tables had been pitiful. Well, one was an antique with hand-painted flowers on it and pleasant to look at though small. It was light and rickety and too small for more than four people.

In our old home that table was perfect because the old home was so sorry. One time we had a guest at the table in our tiny house say, "I feel like I'm on a boat!"

He was looking – from the dining-room table – at the bathroom door frame only a few feet away. It was so angled when it should have been parallel to the ground that his mind told him he was at sea. Probably the small space and gliding table helped complete the picture.

Our kitchen table was no more than a glorified card table. Not quite an antique, it was probably a 1950s or '60s model, all white with three good legs and one whose screw had wallered out the particle board.

We hadn't been at the old farm for more than a year and were sitting at that kitchen table having breakfast, when the exposed wires coming down to the wall outlet sparked and caught on fire not two feet from my head! We put out the little fire and re-wired the house that afternoon.

Just as we knew – after eighteen years in that old farmhouse – that we wanted a reliable house in so many ways, we also knew we wanted a large, solid, non-wiggling table.

"Could you make another table like this one?" we asked Henry.

"Why, yes, I suppose I could," he said with a smile.

Then an idea hit him. "Say, didn't you buy some of Norman Ropp's land?"

"Yes we did," we replied, happy to be recognized and hopeful that the rest of what he knew about us was on the plus side.

"The wood in this table came from trees harvested on that farm about seven years ago."

"It did?!" We were shocked, elated, and hooked.

"Well...do you have any more?"

"Why, yes, I do."

We asked the price and it was fair, of course, though he probably could have added another zero and still made the sale.

We contracted with Henry for a big dining room table of lumber from our land and for cabinets from practically one end of the house to the other: kitchen cabinets, drawers, counters, sinks, and pantries; hall cabinets, counters, and cupboards; bathroom vanity, drawers, counter, sink, and our custom commode. It was a sizable order that would take him quite some time to prepare.

We popped in at Henry's shop from time to time to see where we were in line and to admire his latest work. We were hopeful that the timing of the cabinets would mesh with the rest of the house. On one visit Henry gave us some shocking news.

"We'll be moving down to Windsor, Missouri, this fall."

Amish families, so down to earth and practical and efficient in many regards, have this one annoying habit that I can't figure out. They love to move!

At the drop of a straw hat they'll pack everything up on hired trucks and trailers and move to another community 100, 200, or 500 miles away. What was wrong with the old place? Nothing!

They left behind lovingly worked gardens, bird houses and fences and yard plantings. They left neighbors, relatives, and friends.

To most people, there is a loss of security in moving homes. It's traumatic for children who have to make new friends, go to new schools, and learn new areas. My family moved from Kansas City to Manila, Philippines when I was thirteen and my world turned upside down. It was a hard adjustment for me, I didn't do as well in school, and took a long time to make friends.

But none of that applies to the Amish.

They move to a place that has a school exactly like the last one. Same dress code, same curriculum, same holidays, same school bus (their own two feet or a pony and small buggy if they live farther away). Friends and relatives are probably already there and the new neighbors will soon be good friends that share chores and home church meetings and become part of their daily lives.

When Amish friends moved away, there was nothing at all wrong with the place they left behind that I could see. The houses were big enough for the family, the businesses were good – some very good, so why did the Amish move?

It was never a company transfer or a promotion to the corporate office or something else job related (the only reason my family ever moved except once when we moved two houses down the block in Kansas City) and never to move to warmer or colder climates. It completely baffled me and I never asked about it.

But as I came to understand the priorities of an Amish family, I think I saw the pattern that explained the moves. It was astounding when I thought about it, but perfectly logical for the Amish.

Community decisions are reviewed by the Church bishops basically to see how they stack up against one key question: How will this affect the children? The decision to use automatic milking machines in the dairies weighed the economic benefits against the extra time available to the youth who did the chores. Accepting automatic milkers signaled a more progressive community with more leisure time, which probably didn't sit well with some folks.

Having a tavern in town and an active group of youth in their Rumspringa (running around) days was like matches and gasoline, some folks thought. Although Amish parents are amazingly permissive with their youth during Rumspringa, the Jamesport youth alarmed their parents with their partying prowess.

The Amish youth parties were legendary to me until I actually had first hand experience with several. The first took place in Poosey Conservation Area just to the south of us. A boom box blasted music for most of two days and a neighbor said there was a stream of buggies and pick-ups going in and out. We later saw the party site: a giant bonfire, a few stray cans and bottles not cleaned up, and telltale bare spots around trees where the horses had been tied.

I thought it was a fascinating contrast with their strict upbringing. I, too, was a rebellious youth and caused my parents a lot of grief. I was never into drugs or alcohol but I did want to experience the world at an early age. Sneaking out of the house to take a cab to downtown Manila with my buddy – at the age of fourteen – brought the iron glove down on me. In a city where American youth were kidnapped for ransom (this happened to a friend's sister), my parents probably were scared to death over my empty bed.

Having lived oversees fueled my interest in and appreciation of other cultures, I suppose. Maybe it's my innate curiosity, but, for whatever reason, I'm fascinated by the Amish. That the Amish are a very successful community is remarkable to me. To hold so much of the world at an arm's distance is both admirable and an incredible temptation.

I remembered how I longed to "get out" as a youth – my parents were the strictest among all my friends – and I thought the Amish kids must really have some pent up energy to blow off. I found out first hand one night, driving home from Jamesport at dusk.

*David Schafer*

A horse on the road ahead was misbehaving so I slowed down. This is something drivers in Amish communities are aware of and it's not a big deal. As I approached I saw two young boys on the horse riding bareback. I passed very slowly and one of them waved for me to stop.

I pulled over. I didn't recognize either boy, but I thought they were probably Amish boys dressed in their "English" clothes. One came to the passenger window.

"Can you give one of us a ride?" he asked. "The horse is acting up."

"Sure," I said. "Where you headed?"

"Just down to the railroad tracks."

Hmmm. This was going to be interesting.

We drove the mile to the railroad tracks and he pointed me through the gate onto the railroad right-of-way. Why I didn't notice or even think about going onto private property, I have no idea, but I was about to see my first Amish party in action.

We drove down along the tracks until we came upon a bonfire surrounded by a group of buggies. I stopped a little distance away and my passenger thanked me for the ride.

I saw several kids I knew well. They all came up to say hi like it was no big deal I was there – even though I was a good friend of their parents. From what I saw it looked pretty tame. There was a boom box playing country songs and kids in jeans and sweatshirts hanging around talking and drinking. How long they had been there I don't know but these parties typically lasted several days.

One of my favorite young men, Andrew, came up to the car.

"Hi David! It's my birthday!"

"No kidding. How old are you, Andrew?"

"Eighteen," he said with a big smile.

"Well, have a piece of pizza for a birthday present from me." Alice was away as a working student at a horse farm in Kansas and I'd picked up a pizza for dinner.

Andrew hopped in the front seat. "Don't mind if I do."

We spoke a while. It would be the last time I saw Andrew alive. He and his brothers and father had a pallet shop and had made pallets for me when I first started selling chicken-processing equipment. It was always a joy to walk into the bustle of their shop. The boys gave me huge grins. These were great kids.

Andrew had grown up a lot since then and he was now spreading his wings. I only remember one thing from that conversation and that is how much Andrew admired his older brother, Abe.

"He never took a drink in his life," Andrew told me, a beer in his hand. It might have been the only thing he said without a winning smile that evening. One part of Andrew wanted to please his family and community and be just like his older brother. Another part of him wanted to taste freedom.

Two months later, at a similar party, Andrew was riding a horse, fell into a pond, and never came up. It was a tragedy in the local community, but I think Andrew found the freedom he sought.

He was still sitting in my car when the deputy pulled up behind us and busted the party. At first not much changed. The deputy said he'd had a call from the railroad and wanted us to clear out. The "us" weighed heavily on me. I was now an accessory to a crime, possibly suspected of providing alcohol to minors.

I knew I could not casually drive off the way I'd come in, though several pick-ups were headed out that way.

For the first time, I got out of my car and watched the "bust" unfold. Slowly the kids just scattered into the surrounding woods. More deputies showed up as did the sheriffs of Daviess and Grundy County. I was especially happy to see Greg Coon, Grundy County Sheriff, whom I'd known for fifteen years.

The other deputies and sheriff were younger and didn't know me. The first one asked me to watch a youth he'd put in handcuffs – an unnecessary action, I thought. Another deputy came along and told me to stand somewhere else, which I did. In the meantime the handcuffed kid I was watching snuck off.

"Where'd he go? He's got my handcuffs!" the first deputy shouted when he returned. Later the kid was found in a buggy, handcuffs and all. These kids were not convicts but the Daviess department was out to set an example. The kids were smart enough to party in Grundy County, but stupid enough to taunt the officers from the bushes.

"Go back to Daviess County," they mocked. There were tensions built up that needed some relaxing and I could see that this event only wound the spring tighter. It was all very disorganized until Greg finally showed up and took charge.

"Hi David," he said to me in passing. "You can go."

That was it. I felt under enough suspicion that I really wanted to tell my story beginning with the unruly horse on highway F, but I was happy just to drive off, name cleared or not. I later stopped in at the courthouse to tell them my story.

The party scene drives the Amish parents a little nuts. It certainly doesn't represent their community values in any way. They probably think it gives their community a bad reputation. Andrew's death brought an increased level of intensity to the situation – not only in Jamesport but in Amish communities across the country.

Rumspringa is based on the eloquent philosophy, "Hold a bird too tightly and you'll smother it; hold it too loosely and it will fly away." The parents understand this and are willing to tolerate quite a bit so as to not smother their youth. Until the young adult decides for himself or herself whether or not to join the church there can be quite a bit of anxiety on both parts.

Helping the youth stay in the Amish is so important to the community that it is the foundation of their decision-making process. I also believe it is what causes some folks to pack up and move. The parents see the pitfalls their future teenagers will have to face and want that period to be less traumatic for them.

I have no idea whether that's why Henry Schrock and his family moved but it wouldn't surprise me if it played a part in the decision. Our project was Henry's last installation in Jamesport, making it very important that we should be ready for Henry when he was ready for us.

We had to completely finish all walls and floors and ceilings where cabinets were to go. We rushed the ceilings by asking Johnny Kurtz to help mud. After Johnny's amazing performance we quickly painted all the ceilings. The floors were not as easy.

Like the "breathing" straw-bale walls, the floor had some special requirements. First, because the cement floor was our heat sink and would store the heat from the sunlight through the windows, we couldn't cover it with anything like rugs, linoleum, or wood. The sunlight had to go straight into the concrete.

Second, the floor had to pass the low/no maintenance test like everything in the house. With four cats, a dog and two humans traipsing across it daily, there would be dirt, no doubt about it. Daily sweeping and mopping was not part of the plan, so we had to have a surface that would not look dirty when it really was.

Last, it couldn't be too expensive.

We considered tiles because we like the look and they would actually add to the "thermal mass" of the heat sink, storing the heat in the winter (and the cool in the summer) and giving it off slowly to the house during the night (or day). But tiles would show dirt well and they weren't too cheap.

We considered acid-etching the concrete. This really excited us because we have seen some gorgeous floors prepared this way. Jerry Tichenor etched his floors and they were beautiful. I imagined glossy swirls of copper and emerald that had a regal but not too ostentatious appearance. With the diversity of color and pattern, dirt would hide well.

The process is also not cheap, but it lasts a lifetime. The catch on acid-etching is that it uses dangerously toxic material (sort of a no-no for this earth-friendly house).

We decided to go for it, so we asked Jerry to do the job. "Come on, Jerry. Come up for just one day to do the floors. We'll help."

"You don't need me." Jerry said. "You can do it yourself. It's not hard."

We couldn't wheedle Jerry into the job and didn't want to tackle it ourselves.

With Henry's installation date rapidly approaching, we had to come up with something fast. We special-ordered and tested a dozen different stains on sections of concrete that would be hidden by cabinets. Fortunately, we had a lot of those.

Nothing looked good to us.

Somewhere in the search we picked up a video showing sponge rolling to create mottled effects on walls. We thought we could make it work on our floor.

We carefully selected five colors of latex deck and porch paint. Fawn, seagrass, spanish moss, honeycomb... all natural colors that, we thought, would not be an abrupt transition when coming from the outdoors in any season.

The fawn went on first as a solid, background coat. Then, one by one, I rolled on the other colors, each with a separate sponge roller. The colors swirled and blended into a marbled, pattern-less pattern that defies logic at first glance. "Dirt camo" we named our custom color scheme.

We finished the last room in the middle of the night and there was no time to stand back and admire it all. Henry came to install cabinets the next day.

Henry is a square-peg-in-a-square-hole kind of guy: orderly, consistent, everything in its place. Imagine his surprise at the straw-bale walls and dirt camo floor! He took it all in with one big glance around the large kitchen area and, as always, we enjoyed watching the newcomer digest our "alternative" ideas.

He walked over to the long wall that had the plumbing for the kitchen sink coming out, squatted and put his head against the wall as he sighted down the undulating length.

Our enjoyment turned to panic when Henry issued a long, "Hmmmmm…"

"What is it?"

"Well these walls aren't very straight," he announced, matter of factly.

Well, of course not. That was the beauty of it, the uniqueness of it. And actually, for a straw-bale house the walls were incredibly straight. We'd spent a lot of time with the spade whacking home runs at the bumps until very few remained. Joyce Tichenor saw the walls and remarked that Jerry's were never that straight.

But the cabinets! What were we going to do with the gaps between the wall and the cabinets!? Why hadn't we foreseen this?

Henry stayed cool and offered some ideas. He could add some backing to the splash guards to fit the gaps and then caulk around them. It was a noble offer but would look goofy.

Then Alice got way out of the box.

"We'll knock out some of the walls!"

"What?!" I said.

"We'll just tear into the walls on the high spots and set the cabinets in."

There was something about the words, "tear into the walls" that my brain refused to process. Maybe it had to do with destroying parts of the walls that we'd plastered over – how many was it now? – about six times!

Alice was already seeing it happen and full of excitement at the prospect of destroying chunks of our kitchen wall to make a flush surface. Henry was nodding his head in agreement. Alice already had a hammer and chisel out before I regained my powers of speech.

She tore into the walls with as much glee as she had with the first coat of mud. Like an archeologist, she uncovered the recent layers of our lives. Through the yellowish layer of drywall joint compound (mud), through the white layer, into the greenish-brown sandy mud, back to the browner mud with straw, and into the chocolate-covered-pretzels of the outer straw bale and, finally, into pure straw.

We measured, whittled, measured, and whittled some more. Finally, we slid the long bank of cabinets snuggly up against the wall. A few areas would need some drywall mud to be tapered down to the splash guard, but it was not a big deal. Hardly noticeable.

In less than half an hour after my brain seizure, Henry was efficiently assembling all the cabinets and pantries, base boards and splashguards, securing the cabinets to interior walls and the cedar 2 x 6s under the bottom bales. Almost like he would in any other, normal house.

# CHAPTER 10
# OFF THE ROOF

R ICHARD MORRIS SHOWED us the old well site on the farm; he had known about it as a kid since he grew up there. Norman Ropp also showed us the well on his property. Norman's was still in use. Rumor had it that it was the only well in the immediate area to not go dry in severe drought years.

We knew a little bit about wells since Grandpa had dug one on the old farm. It was several hundred feet deep and we never used it. It probably cost Grandpa a lot of money.

On the other hand, I counted seven old, hand-dug, limestone rock-lined wells on the old farm and most still had good water in them.

The old farm had a huge cistern that collected water off the roof of the big house – a common practice before public water systems – and that system appealed to us for several reasons.

First, we wanted one big, multi-purpose out-building to house our tractor, truck, car and shop. That shed would be big enough to catch a lot of rain water, about 1000 gallons per inch of rain as it turned out on a 30' x 90' roof.

Second, we wouldn't have to run a pump to collect it. Gravity would do the work.

Third, a cement cistern could be poured under the shop area of the shed. This would support the shop floor, share walls with a root cellar/oil changing pit, and the cistern roof would be the shop floor sharing another wall. That was efficient use of concrete.

We conservatively figured our water needs at 100 gallons a day – an impossible figure for us to use since our Maytag washer only uses 13 gallons per load, a bath 20 gallons at the most (compared to about 5 for a shower) and our toilets zero since they are composting.

With a sixty-day period of no rain – about the most we would expect in north Missouri – 6000 gallons of storage seemed plenty. That's about what an 8' x 16' room seven feet high provided. We decided to split the area in half to make two reservoirs each holding 3000 gallons. That way, we could clean one while drawing from the other.

The shed sits sixty feet from the house and about six feet higher in elevation so that when the cisterns are full the water level is equal to head height in the house and gravity brings it down. But unlike pressure from fifty or sixty-foot tall water towers, five feet is not nearly enough pressure for showering or washing clothes.

We had to boost the pressure somehow. And we found just the way to do it.

In the course of studying different natural building materials and alternative energy sources, we ran into Rob Roy several times. He built a house out of cordwood and cement that looked easy, efficient and inexpensive. We had been attracted to Scott and Helen Nearing's slip-form stone construction. The cordwood masonry used lighter weight natural materials (wood) that were easier to collect, and could be made thick enough to provide great insulation. The look was interesting and pleasant.

In a Home Power video Rob made - mostly talking about the solar system in his cordwood masonry house – there was a brief segment showing Rob riding a stationary bicycle to pump his house water. I watched it over and over again but couldn't figure it out completely.

I called Rob and he put me on to his friend who designed it, George Barber. It sounded simple in principle. You mate a "turned around" bicycle to a piston pump.

While looking for a junked bike, I stumbled first into an exercise bike and realized it was perfect for the job since the drive chain already went forward to the front wheel instead of the back. I wouldn't have to "turn around" the bike by swapping seat for handle bars. Buying the virtually new exercise bike from my buddy, Packrat Pete, for 50 cents was the easiest part of the deal.

I was also lucky sourcing the old piston pumps. Cecil Hobbs knew exactly what I was talking about and made a slow bee-line through the piles of derelict heavy metal in his junkyard to an old truck.

"I think I've got several of them in the cab where they're out of the weather."

He had four. I chose two matching Meyer pumps, their green paint still in good shape, thinking I could afford the investment in the long haul as I'd have parts available. I told Cecil our plan minus the bicycle part.

"Well that's how everybody used to get water pressure in the old days. They all had cisterns and these little pumps."

I asked Cecil what he wanted for them, knowing that George Barber said they were hard to find and cost over $100 there.

"Oh…." Cecil stared at them a second, "does forty dollars sound fair?"

I shook my head yes as I reached in my wallet for eighty dollars. "Each?" I asked just to be sure.

"No, for the pair."

That's one thing I love about north Missouri. Folks selling something always reckon it from the perspective of "what they've got in it" rather than "if you had to buy one new."

How many times I've heard the phrase, "Well, I'd like to get back what I've got in it."

There's an unspoken code of conduct here that frowns on gouging and gives the neighbor a fair deal. I know north Missouri isn't the only last bastion of this practice, but it isn't that common anymore.

Though Cecil kept the pumps out of the weather, they had been baked in the truck cab and everything rubber inside needed to be replaced. I had the fortune of doing open-pump surgery and seeing how the ingenious device worked. With every stroke of the piston – both forward and back – a fist-sized gulp of water was pulled or pushed through the pump, eventually into our bladder tank, another ingenious device.

The bladder tank is a steel tank with water in the bottom section, air in the top and a rubber diaphragm, or bladder, in between. As water is pumped into the lower section it compresses the air above, building pressure. By putting a bicycle chain sprocket on the piston pump and a bladder tank in the water line we could peddle leisurely and have plenty of water pressure in 10 or 15 minutes.

I keep saying I may mount a little ¼ horsepower motor on the pump like they all used to have. But the chore remains a very pleasant one I actually look forward to and we never tire of demonstrating the bike-driven water pump to visitors.

And how many times have I heard the quip, "David, does Alice make you ride the bike when she wants to take a shower?"

"Not often," I'm ready with a grin. "We go by the 'save water, shower with a buddy' system!"

# CHAPTER 11
# OFF THE GRID

WE WOULDN'T HAVE dreamed of clearing a path for power lines along our beautiful drive. Alice flew out to Ukiah, California for a one-day solar power class put on by Real Goods and learned just enough to give her the confidence that solar power was doable.

The house had been built – up to this point – by the power of a seven-kilowatt RV generator my Dad had given us. We knew many people survived on generator power alone, but we were lucky to live in an area with plentiful sunshine so solar power looked like a good option to us.

Even though we had let go of the huge negative influence of the giant hogs – and gone so far as to appreciate their influence in our new phase of life – we still enjoyed snubbing the powerful utilities companies that worked hard to bring the giants in and profited from their massive power consumption.

Basically our new lifestyle and home was a statement of independence and self-reliance. We would be self-sufficient and kowtow to no one. We had decided some years back when Alice had the opportunity to interview with the recently elected Governor, Mel Carnahan, for the position of Director of Agriculture, that we would take the Gandhi approach rather than the Nehru approach.

It gave us a bad case of the heebie-jeebies to imagine living a life of politics at the state capital and trying to make changes from that platform. Alice started losing sleep after Larry Harper, editor of the Missouri Ruralist magazine, told her he thought she had a good chance of being chosen for the position. Alice finally reneged, wrote a letter of regret to Governor Carnahan, and from that moment on our path of influence was clear.

We would lead by example and inspiration. We would craft the best existence we could imagine, choose to be the happiest people we could be, heal the earth with our farming practices, raise the world's happiest livestock, produce the world's healthiest food, and feed the world's nicest, most appreciative people.

Power lines just didn't fit in that picture so we studied solar and wind power and ultimately opted for solar alone. A wind generator requires periodic maintenance and the state of the technology at that time was not advanced.

It took us a long time to let go of the wind-generator idea. In fact, we had one ordered and delivered but never unpacked it and finally sent it back. I drew plan after plan of 80-foot towers that were hinged and lowered by cable to do the servicing. I considered parking a junked crane in the middle of the pasture. All we needed was one with the cable winch still operational. That would make turbine maintenance easy.

Wind turbines fit many alternative power supplies but they didn't fit ours. For back-up power during periods of cloudy weather we could rely on the generator.

It's easy to look only at the economics of solar vs. power company electricity but there are two additional factors to consider: Safety and reliability. Alice and I were clearing brush and small trees under a power line along our property one day when Alice felled a small tree that barely caught the power line. It made a connection to the earth and lit the place up like the Fourth of July for about a minute.

We backed away in horror as sparks flew and the power line burned in two and fell to the ground. Oops! We hurried back to the house to report it to the utility company and found they had already received dozens of phone calls from neighbors who had lost their power.

The unreliability of being cut off from service because of an accident like that or a lightening storm or a high use brown-out is merely an inconvenience. But then consider all the severe burns and lives lost from electrocution due to accidentally coming in contact with those high-voltage wires.

That's not to say solar-generated power isn't dangerous. It's just as dangerous as 110-volt current in any house and care must be exercised around the battery box. But there are no extremely dangerous high-voltage overhead wires to worry about.

Besides safety and reliability concerns, there are serious social and environmental considerations that cannot be ignored in the production of electricity from coal. The relatively cheap cost of electricity generated from the burning of coal or the operation of nuclear power plants doesn't include the hidden costs of pollution and contamination. Nor does it factor in the costs of sickness and death in the event of a nuclear plant accident or a transportation accident involving coal or radioactive materials. You just don't have those risks with home-generated solar power.

For all those reasons we favored solar power, yet it was still a huge unknown to us. We knew no one who used it and we weren't sure all of our appliances – computers, refrigerator, copy machine, telephones – would work with it.

Basically, the idea is to convert solar energy to electricity in panels and store it in a battery bank. But battery banks don't come in 110 volts, they come in 12 and 24 and 48 volts, so the juice needs to change shape coming out of the battery bank in order to operate normal household appliances. This is done with an expensive piece of equipment called an inverter.

Inverters do a good job of changing the electricity from 12 or 24 volt to 110 volt, but they aren't perfect. Sometimes normal appliances won't run on inverted power.

We might not have had the guts to go through with the project if it hadn't been for Lonnie Gamble in Fairfield, Iowa. Besides welcoming us to his extremely cool straw-bale house and teaching us how to mix mud plaster properly, Lonnie is an energy consultant and offered to make the four-hour drive to help install our solar system. Seeing his place function so easily boosted our confidence and tipped the scales.

To prepare for Lonnie's arrival, Alice, who from the start took the lead on the solar electricity, built a box to house our 12 golf-cart batteries. Small PVC pipes exit the battery box, enter an interior house wall, and run up to the attic to vent any battery gases produced.

We scrounged through Cecil's junkyard again and fashioned an adjustable rack of light-weight but strong aluminum to hold the panels. Alice measured and drilled holes so that we could bolt the rack at three different angles to the sun.

In the winter when the sun averages 45 degrees off the horizon, the panels are set at 55 degrees from horizontal to make a right angle to the sun. Conversely, in the summer when the sun appears only 20 degrees south of vertical, the panels are set at a right angle to that, lying relatively flat. For spring and fall there are settings half way between these two.

We met Lonnie at the old farm and I hopped in his car and guided him to the new house. As we crested the hill of our driveway and the house came into view, Lonnie said, "Wow, look at that! A stone-walled, straw-bale home!"

Endearing him to me forever, Lonnie took out his movie camera and filmed the house out of one eye as he drove slowly up the driveway, all the time gushing about how beautiful our house was. Like us, Lonnie is a big fan of Scott and Helen Nearing, the "good life" pioneers, and appreciated all the Nearings did by themselves with stone.

"I don't think anyone has ever covered a straw-bale house with stone," Lonnie said.

A permaculture teacher and energy consultant with bases in Iowa and Hawaii, and contacts all over the world, Lonnie would probably know.

Since Lonnie had taught us the fundamentals of mixing mud plaster and had given us the confidence to build our own straw-bale home, he rightly felt paternal toward our house project. Working hands-on to give electrical life to the house, Lonnie augmented his considerable influence and instilled more of his beautiful spirit in our house.

At the end of the day we had electricity without the familiar drone of the generator and without ugly, dangerous power lines coming to the house.

We plugged in the appliances one by one. The Vestfrost refrigerator's lights came on; the compressors rattled and settled into a happy, working hum. The Maytag Neptune clothes washer seemed happy. We turned it off and headed for the office. The first computer booted up fine. Second computer booted up fine. The Canon copier blinked and shut off with a flashing error message. We tried again and the same thing happened.

Well, if we had to choose one appliance of all those to be unhappy, it would have been the copier. I say this despite the fact that, over the years, we had become surprisingly dependent on our home copier. It saved us money and time-consuming trips to town on many occasions. Would we have to get rid of it?

We called Trace, the inverter manufacturer, and received remarkably good news.

"Just go to your local electric supply store and buy a $15 line filter and put it in a line anywhere in the house."

"Any line?"

"Any line."

"Just splice it in?"

"Just splice it in."

"Only $15?"

"Only $15."

Phone geeks make patience an art form.

"What does it do?"

"It takes the edges off the sine wave the inverter puts out."

Right. Made perfect sense. We bought a line filter for about $15, spliced it on a line and the copier purred and made copies.

That was the extent of fine tuning required to put us totally in the business of converting sunshine to ice cubes, fluorescent light, clean clothes, computer messages, and crisp copies.

# CHAPTER 12
# GOOD TO GO

I N HIS SEVENTEEN years with us, Buckley achieved an unusual amount of notoriety for a dog. He appeared in magazine and book cover photos, postcards, Christmas cards, sweatshirts and paintings. Ever the humble one, he had not volunteered for a single one of those glamour spots.

It was always his doting people, Alice and I, who insisted Buck be photographed. For every photo that exists showing any part of Buck's face, there are a dozen showing the back of his head as he stares up at us ready for the next task after coming. Occasionally one of us would put our rear to the camera, ask Buck to sit and stay, give him some "Good boys," and quickly assume a position behind him for a "family photo" or happy farm scene. Ever true to character, Buck doted on us and tried his best to please, but turning his back on us was very disruptive to his spirit not to mention hard on his neck. Sometimes he could hold the pose for a frame or two but more often he is facing us.

Well sure, most of those photographic appearances are because we drug him out to share our limelight as big fish in the shrinking pond of human-scale agriculture. But we wouldn't have considered otherwise, so big a role did Buck have in our life. He was there for everything between 1989 and 2006.

He came in with our first sheep and Jenny the Guard Donkey and G.P. the Great Pyrenees dog. He helped us raise goats, pigs and chickens and was a key player in the refined grazing of cattle we practiced. His job was the most important and dangerous one of the three of us. Heck, all we had to do was open the gate. He was the one charged with the task of preventing the exuberant cattle from wastefully dashing to the end of the pastures and back. He was admired by visitors on farm tours and loved by all family members whether they could throw a Frisbee or not.

He walked the new Poosey property and the adjacent conservation area with us, always scouting ahead, and easily transitioned to it from the farm he had always known. As my walks became slower in the woods, Buck understood and walked behind me, putting my desire to encounter the wildlife ahead of his own to explore.

All three of us grew comfortably into our separate roles at the new farm we dubbed "Wonderland." Alice devoted herself to horsewomanship, training and competing her beloved thoroughbred horses. I devoted myself to a growing business of manufacturing poultry processing equipment and a new old hobby of studying the natural world. Buckley devoted himself to becoming the Wunder Hunder, the Wonder Dog.

He tentatively accepted indoor dog privileges for the last seven years of his life. It was difficult for him to accept that invitation at first but we insisted since he no longer had the warm basement with a doggy door that the big house at the old farm provided. Even so, he never took that privilege for granted. He never came through a door without asking and awaiting an invitation. His respect for our space was immense.

We soon installed a doggy door on our front door and Buckley stepped into that newfound freedom. But that, too, he passed through tentatively, almost as if knocking. He always flipped the heavy plastic flaps twice with his nose – making a telltale rhythmic 'flap-flap' before walking through.

As all pets do, Buckley found his favored spots in the house. There were several but all had a common denominator: they were within sight of us. When we were both in the office he would plop down just outside the lone office door. When we were at the kitchen table he'd plop down at the west end of it. When we were reading in the living room he'd plop down between us. When we were in bed he'd plop down on one side of it.

If Alice and I were at opposite ends of our long, skinny house, he had to split the difference and park somewhere in the middle. That constituted a tough decision that was decided by who was more active than the other. He stayed near the action.

If we rose from seated to standing, Buck rose too, ready for whatever was next. It's hard for the human mind to grasp that level of trust and devotion. Whatever was our desire was his desire. He lived to serve, to share life experiences with us.

It's funny. Now that he's gone and we miss him, we feel more fully how devoted and full of unconditional love he was. We have commented to each other how easy it is to feel Buck's unique love in his physical absence. I see his penetrating brown eyes, expectant and happy, and a wagging, white-tipped tail in the background.

A hopeful expectancy must surely be a key ingredient to a long, happy life. Buck's faculties began failing long before his spirit, which, in fact, never failed. Buck lost most of his hearing somewhere around 2005. Could it have been from the endless circles that he made "dogging" the farm machinery? For whatever reason he could no longer hear our "Buck" calls or the sound of vehicles. Even in our remote location without passing traffic I worried a bit about that.

An interesting - and logical, I suppose – reaction to hearing loss occurred with Buck. He began to compensate for his lack of connection through sound by coming close to us to be petted. This was new for Buck. He previously showed outright affection rarely – as in the endearing "Buck phone" posture with his head against ours while riding in the car or truck if we were stopped and waiting. Now he began craving our touch and was quite insistent about it. This satisfied his need for connection with us.

It did wear a little thin during a two-year phase of what we called the "Buck alarm." Very early in the morning, around 5 am, we would be awakened by a loud drumming next to the bed. The first time we bolted upright. Then we realized it was Buck, expectantly wagging at the bedside, his tail drumming against the resonant back of the dresser.

I learned to roll over and pat his head while mostly asleep. But when I stopped and pulled my hand back onto the bed the drumming started up again. If I left my hand lazily on his head or back he soon nodded under it to activate me again, an effective snooze button. Really the only way to turn off the Buck alarm for the morning was to get up and prepare his morning feed.

That was my chore and it was an artful breakfast if I do say so. Buckley had an always full bowl of Flint River Ranch Pet Food – a premium quality food that we believed in to the point of becoming dealers for it. But that was dry food and even though oven-baked and shipped to our door for freshness it was still, well, a little boring. To supplement that we fed Buck out of our extensive larder of organ meats from our natural meat business.

He got the $4/pound stuff! Beef, lamb and pork liver, heart, kidney and spleen, occasionally some "fries," Buck had a morning buffet fit for the king of dogs. Along with that offering came some supplement pills and a bone to work over. No wonder he wanted me up early!

As he aged, however, backing up out of the narrow space between the bed and dresser must have become more difficult because the Buck alarm ceased to go off anymore. Even with weakened hips he still was always game for a walk. Some of Alice's training rides were very long and sometimes fast, so out of concern for his stamina Alice painfully put him in the house and locked the doggy door before these particular training rides.

As for me, his slowed pace matched perfectly with mine and we took many long walks in Poosey, sometimes camping in the pines with a little fire and a lean-to shelter. Buck always declined the shelter though; he'd rather lie out in the snow.

For Alice's birthday in 2006 I asked our good friend Loreen, a talented artist, to paint an "intuitive portrait" of Alice, capturing her essence. Loreen took to the idea immediately. It wasn't to be a physical likeness so much as to represent the inner Alice. I offered little guidance. Loreen did sneak out once while Alice was away to look at Alice's new horse barn that meant so much to her.

The finished portrait was presented at a party and I was apprehensive because it would be easy to see if Alice didn't like it although she would certainly be polite and praising. Well. Alice loved it. She couldn't stop raving about it and couldn't walk by it for weeks without stopping and marveling at it. Loreen's genius was simple. She portrayed Alice in a pixyish costume which looked a lot like riding clothes, her hands outstretched in a "Tadah!" pose, barn in the background, Luc on the left, Olympic rings above and Buckley on the right looking up at her.

It was perfection and reflected Loreen's powerful intuition as well as Alice's Wonderland world. In the dream world that Loreen depicted Luc attentively watches Alice, the horse barn rises in the background, lofty goals show in the Olympic aspirations, and in front of it all a Peter Pan-like Alice shines brightly and victoriously.

But why Buckley in Alice's dream world? Long ago a friend told Alice that Buckley was sort of a spiritual escort for her; they had an uncommon attachment. We had told no one of this but Loreen portrayed it exactly as this friend had been given the image in her mind's eye.

What about me? Barely noticeable to one side is a large tree, silent and supportive.

Loreen presented the painting to Alice in early May, two months before Buck's passing as it turned out.

Probably the greatest accolade ever awarded Buck was from Kansas City artist, Marie Mason. Marie and Kate discovered us at the City Market in the early 2000s. Marie passed our booth, glanced at our brag book of photos and impetuously asked, "Can I take this photo home? I promise I'll send it back!"

Who on earth was this person? Kate quickly rescued the scene. "Oh, Marie is an outstanding artist and just wants to paint a picture of your pigs."

Marie loved the notion of pigs in the woods and, being the fierce advocate of animal rights that she is, took a photo home and, to our glee, produced "Porcinicity," a large acrylic of our happy pigs.

That was just the beginning of our relationship with Kate and Marie. Marie's bread and butter is themed shirts and sweatshirts, almost all of dogs. Many organizations have commissioned Marie to produce a theme for them. She has a rare talent for capturing scenes that allow the purity of the animals to convey the sentiment. A glance at her work speaks to you viscerally and immediately. Although she uses color, not line drawings, her work reminded me somehow of James Thurber who was not known for his art but, like his writing, it struck to the heart of the matter at hand.

After completing Porcinicity, Marie visited us on several occasions and later used a photo she took of Buckley to create a rendering of him in his "down" position. It is a position used in shepherding to control the pressure on the sheep. Although down, the dog is far from passive. He is focused, expectant, alert and very much on call. Marie had the painting done several weeks before the caption came to her. She sent an email and what came to me was "devotion." That was close and Marie allowed that it was a good title.

The next thing I knew there were t-shirts out with Buckley on them captioned "Good to go." That was it. The genius of the artist is to plumb the depths and draw out the essence of their subject. Bingo. Buck epitomized "good to go" and now he was the poster dog for it. The family all got "Good to go" tee shirts for Christmas.

Buck was good to go right up to his last hours. Even though he had been losing weight and his muscles weakened he still made forays into the woods nearby just for fun. One afternoon after Alice's horse ride we couldn't find Buck in the house or the barn where he was when she left. I searched for nearly two hours before thinking that he might just be totally disoriented and following a downhill course. I walked downhill from the barn to the edge of the woods in a draw at our property fence and stood with my hands on my hips. Now where to look? I stood for perhaps a minute and was in the process of turning back toward the house when a movement caught my eye.

Down in the bottom of the ravine in the neighbor's woods was Buck looking confused and facing away from home. I could see that he had overcome several obstacles to get where he was, probably stumbling many times as he was doing more and more lately. I walked up to where he could smell me and waited for him to turn. I had played this game with him for years, hiding in the woods until he found me with his incredible nose. I had also learned that an unexpected touch on the back – even a gentle one – would cause a yelp of fear and probably a fall.

As soon as he scented me, saw me and registered a little recognition I scooped him up and carried him uphill. His rear was covered with green flies. Were they sensing death or was it just the diarrhea he recently suffered? Alice called and I told her I had him. We carried him together and Alice bathed him.

We were on full alert with Buck after that; a few days later he had the first of four seizures. After each except the last he would come back and eventually get up and walk around again. We took shifts spending the night with him, sleeping on an air mattress by his side petting him and cleaning him. By dawn Alice had had enough and didn't want him to have to live this way any longer. He had lived a long life and the quality was gone. The sooner his struggle was over the better.

I agreed that he was on the way out but didn't feel his life should end quite that soon. This impasse brought us to a height of emotion the likes of which we hadn't unleashed on each other for years. Finally, to strike a truce we decided to call upon an animal communicator to ask Buck if he wanted assistance. The fifth number Alice dialed reached a woman named Karen who took our call even though she was just sitting down to a restaurant lunch. She went out to her van to quiet her mind so she could connect with Buck.

We were not surprised when she told us that she, too, was saying goodbye to a long-time animal companion. She laid out some groundwork in the discussion, mostly to break the ice, and we listened patiently, knowing how the process worked since we had taken a few classes in animal communication years ago. Basically, you relax and open up to messages in whatever form they may take – pictures, words, symbols. Alice and I make a practice of being open to guidance from the natural world much as native peoples the world over have always done. But we felt too close to the situation and emotionally wrought to trust ourselves to read Buckley completely accurately.

After exclaiming about the depth of our connection with this dog and the extraordinary energy he had, Karen finally got to the question.

"He is happy either way, to go naturally or with assistance. It doesn't matter to him. The main thing is that he wants you present. He does say that there may be some 'herking and jerking' that may be alarming if he goes naturally. But it's up to you to decide who can better live with the compromise."

We thanked her profusely and settled in with her words, Buck's words. In the relaxing of the tension that brought I grabbed a few minutes at the computer to catch up with business. Alice came in, near tears, accusing me of not being present with Buckley.

"I think she meant 'in the present moment' when we're with him," I countered.

"No. She meant present with him. How can you be here when he wants you with him?" she said, tears flowing freely now.

Oh dear, we're not resolved yet. I had been toying with the idea of setting a time, like sundown, when we would assist his transition, but I hadn't had the courage to propose it yet. Since Karen's phone call Alice was satisfied Buck wasn't suffering and wasn't in a hurry to leave his body, but it was very hard on her to have no plan of action.

I finally suggested I call Dr. Jim Colyer to schedule him at the end of his work day. She agreed. It took me another hour to make the phone call.

We hadn't called on Dr. Jim for years; in fact, he'd never been to our new farm. We had very little need for a veterinarian lately. But I chose Dr. Jim for his humanity. He and I had shared a heart-wrenching event together once before and I knew his character; he would honor this situation as we wished it to unfold.

Years ago we had made the mistake of letting some pregnant heifers have the run of the "back" pasture, almost 200 acres of woods and meadows.

We noticed a heifer trying to calve unsuccessfully and I asked Alice to call the vet as I gathered up the equipment to assist her.

Well, the heifer wasn't wild but she just wouldn't let me get close enough to drop a lariat around her neck. I slowly walked the farm with her for several hours before a lucky long throw caught her head. I quickly looped my end around a tree. I set to work with sleeves and strap to find the feet and present the fetus properly. It was a huge calf in a terrible presentation. I tried and tried to gently bring the errant hooves forward with the heifer clamping on my arm the whole time. Although I had a fair amount of experience at this it wasn't going well.

Incredibly, Jim walked out of the woods.

"How on earth did you find us?" I asked.

"I've been looking for two hours," Jim replied. Not every vet would do that.

He quickly took over and assessed the situation as hopeless. The calf was already dead and the mother was bleeding badly internally. I felt terrible that I had caused the bleeding but Jim adamantly disputed the point, saying the calf did it.

Having no anesthesia, and with my agreement, he used a scalpel to sever her carotid artery and put her out of her misery. I was wrung out emotionally and we both shed tears as she slowly gave up the ghost.

"Hi Jim. This is David Schafer."

"Hi David."

"Jim, I have a solemn task I'd like you to help us with." I hoped he didn't hear the catch in my voice.

Silence.

"Could you come out here at the end of your work day and assist Buckley in passing on?"

He asked me for the particulars of Buck's state and he said he'd be there at 6 or 6:30.

That gave us three to three and a half hours with Buck. Everything changed immediately after that. All tension lifted. We were totally aligned with the eventuality and settled in to the glorious task of celebrating those upcoming 10 to 12,000 seconds.

How can I describe what a gift it is to know the exact amount of time a loved one has remaining? Not a thought of "how long will that last?" clouded our minds; that was resolved. We were free to focus 100% on the task of appreciating this glorious being for the last moments we would share with him physically.

The day had been cloudy, cool and drizzly and I'd set a pavilion tent over us for protection. Alice and I lay on air mattresses on either side of Buck in the front yard – where he last fell – and communed. One or both of us petted him constantly. He was very expressive, had his head up from time to time and seemed to suffer no pain.

At six o'clock he had another seizure that lasted almost a minute. With muscles contracted he couldn't breathe and I thought surely this was it but he slowly came back, breathing heavily at first and then normally. After that he lay on his side but watched us with his eyes and moved his head around.

Dr. Jim arrived at 7:00 and with very few words it was over. Alice held Buckley in her arms looking into his eyes and sobbing as I followed Jim back to his truck.

"I can write you a check now if you like - "

"No check. No fee," Jim cut me off with a wave of finality.

"Peace," he said, and turned and left.

I joined Alice and we let the tears flow. After a while I left to dig a grave in the woods. We carried Buck in a red cotton cloth with two big sunflower heads our dear neighbor Patti brought from the patch growing in Poosey directly across from her house. Alice added some button flowers from her garden. A long limestone rock – left from our house construction – protruded from the grave as a marker.

At the grave we each said a few words. Some of the bright yellow petals of the sunflowers had come off and we sprinkled them over the red cloth. Remembering that green was the third Native American power color to go with red and yellow (symbolic of the eagle nation), I impulsively grabbed some leaves from a nearby plant and sprinkled their green color over the red and yellow. The leaves were about the size of a quarter and beautifully oval and seemed the perfect addition before we covered our old friend with earth.

At dawn the next morning while I marveled at the perfection of Buck's love, the inspiration of his life, and the beauty of his passing, an amazing synchronicity revealed itself to me. I walked out to the grave and looked closely at the plant whose leaves I had borrowed. Sure enough. In that final impulse to complete the color triad that would send Buck soaring with eagles, we had unknowingly adorned his body with leaves of the species Symphoricarpos orbiculatus, known in some areas as Coralberry or Indian Currant. But around here everybody calls it… Buckbrush.

# Chapter 13
## Lucky Years - Marketing

WE DIDN'T KNOW the lambs we bought at the Tina sale barn in the spring of 2004 would be our last batch of lambs. Nor could we have known that we would get a pet lamb out of the deal. Sometimes it's best not to know too much in advance.

For ten years the City Market in downtown Kansas City had been the answer to our dreams. We began attending tentatively in 1994, appearing unannounced and in random stalls with our product under ice in coolers. I had had to fight hard to get in. The Market Manager said they didn't have any meat vendors and I'd have to get clearance from the KC Health Department.

I found out that the current Health Department regulations regarding meat sales at the City market were written before refrigeration existed! They stated that meats could be sold only between the months of October and March. In other words, when it was cold outside. We wanted to sell year round.

The voice at the other end of the phone was all bureaucrat. I had been passed along several times and hoped this woman had the authority to make a decision. I pointed out that our meats would all be inside freezers so they would be colder than meats outdoors between October through March. There was a long pause as she figured out what to do with me.

"You'll have to be established as a truck vendor and have to purchase a truck vendor's license and you'll have to have thermometers in the freezers showing that they are below freezing."

"Yes ma'am!" I was happy to say.

The ridiculous $275 annual truck license covered the cost of inspectors peeking in our freezer to read the thermometers – a safety precaution that occurred exactly twice in ten years. As it turned out, it took more than two months to pay off the first year's license fee.

We were lucky to make $200 a day those first few months. The profit would be about $20 after subtracting fuel and market stall fees. We persevered and improved our packaging and display. We were the first meat vendors in the first Wild Oats store in KC and proudly displayed a sign saying so at our market stall.

We got to know the other vendors, the market manager, and the permanent shopkeepers. Mostly we got to know our customers. Since we could bring only a limited supply we often ran out of things and quickly started the practice of taking a notebook and asking folks if they wanted us to bring them something in particular on our next Saturday "just so they could be sure to get it."

That appealed to our customers. We took their names and phone numbers (for a reminder call) and the business grew.

In a few short years the freezer was filled mostly with orders so we cut our hours from all day to just two hours, 8 to 10 am. If the customer didn't show we offered their goodies at 10 am and went home. Only two hours at market whittled it down to a six-hour venture counting travel time. We added another freezer and soon had it filled with orders also. We added a hydraulic lift tailgate to get the freezers on and off the truck and squeezed in a third, small freezer.

It became clear to us that we could make a living on a very small acreage with this business and that led to moving to the Wonderland property and a whole new chapter of deliberate living on a small farmstead.

So how could it come to pass that after only five years on our new homestead we were considering dropping the reins of the meat business? It wasn't an easy conclusion to reach. In fact, we were pretty thickheaded there for a while and poor Lucky suffered as a result.

The good news was that my partnership with Amish neighbors to manufacture small-farm-scale poultry-processing equipment was turning out to be successful. Our sales had already eclipsed our best year's meat sales for two years running. That success removed our economic need to continue meat marketing.

The first bit of bad news was the City Market itself. The management had changed for the worse and though we were still friendly, they imposed some regulations that were particularly hard on our customers and us. Because a delivery truck had hit one of their employees they instigated changes, probably demanded by insurance, that prohibited drive-through traffic at the market.

Since many orders weighed 50 pounds or more, that was hard on our customers. Some folks got hundreds of pounds of meat all at once. With the new regulations, we had to help cart it one to three blocks away to their cars. We bought a little red wagon to help with the job.

But worse than that inconvenience, they wouldn't let us drive in at 8 and leave at 10 any more. No exceptions! The market opened at 7 am and closed at 2 pm, meaning vehicle traffic was prohibited during those hours.

We were prisoners! Never mind that many of our two-dozen patrons per visit came there primarily to meet us and were strong shoppers at other stalls. We had zero clout. It wasn't about customer or vender safety; it was about insurance and avoiding litigation.

Proof of that came the next year with the abominable letter stating that all vendors had to have $5 million in insurance coverage for the following year! Added to that, the City Market insisted that five of their business entities be named on our insurance policies.

Easy-going humans that we are, we at first said okay, we'll play your game and make the best of it. We got up early again and found other things to do for the four extra hours in the city (still asking our customers to arrive in the two-hour window). After a season of that nonsense we resolved to find a new venue, and the insurance letter sealed that resolution.

The second big sticker was Kramer's freezer. Having a place to store our meat had been a weak link in our business ever since we left the old farm and our thirteen deep-chest freezers behind. Solar power on our new farm didn't support one freezer let alone thirteen. Over the life span of our business we've stored our meats in several business lockers, a friend's walk-in, and our own freezers. None of them were perfect solutions.

When Vernon Kramer added a freezer on to his dry-goods store and told me how big it was going to be I marveled that he could do that with diesel power and asked if he was going to rent locker space. I got in line with other happy neighbors to reap the benefits of another Amish entrepreneur boldly going where others (me, foremost) feared to go.

Oh, it's not that we never considered building our own freezer. We invested a lot of time and energy into studying it. We even agreed to buy a freezer from a Kansas City locker that was going out of business but when we began dismantling it we found the panels were solid blocks of ice and had lost their insulating ability. That permanently spooked us; the solar home removed any lingering hopes.

A freezer in the community – still a 12-minute drive one way – was another prayer answered. We nestled into a corner of the freezer as soon as it was cold. Never mind that it was dark as a dungeon and we were right under the two behemoth compressors that sounded like jet engines firing up when they kicked in.

With folding tables, cardboard boxes, plastic bags, magic markers, calculators, thick gloves, warm coats and caps and ear plugs, we'd pull boxes of beef, lamb, chicken and pork and fill orders into other boxes and bags and load them into freezers on the back of our truck. This was Friday afternoon's chore from hell. It never took less than two hours, often four or more. As usual, Alice was the brain, I was the brawn.

And I'm embarrassed to say I wilted under the pressure. Cold and fatigue and increasingly longer order lists led to something less than my best outlook on life. Alice strengthened and grew taller under the stress; I counted the minutes and dreamt of quiet, sunny beaches. I dreaded the chore despite the good money and noble service it represented.

And, as if the cold, noise, and physical fatigue of lifting dozens of frozen, fifty-pound boxes weren't enough, a huge ice flow began developing in our corner. The compressor's condensation was supposed to drain out through exit tubes but continually froze inside the room, dripping down the freezer walls and spreading like a cold and hungry virus across the floor and into our storage racks.

We raised boxes. We chipped ice. We put grit on the floor to keep from slipping. We walked very carefully.

We gently mentioned it to Becky, Vern's wife, though we needn't have. She knew. Vern knew. It was driving them both crazy too. Vern chipped the ice out several times too. His quick-chill room, with its own compressor working twice as hard as the two in our corner, was even worse.

Becky did graciously show us how to turn the compressors off while we were working inside. We always managed to remember to turn them back on, but one day we left with the garage door into the freezer wide open. (Violation of farm rule #1: Close the gate.) I guess Vern found out during his Saturday morning chores. We wanted to pay for the extra diesel fuel used but Vern wouldn't hear of it.

I wasn't looking forward to another season of fighting the cold, my fatigue, and the ice, but I ignored those feelings. Instead we were planning a new approach – the buying club idea. Every farmer's market we considered in Kansas City had deal-squashing problems so we decided to side-step them completely.

We would draft a handful of "host" customers; make deliveries to their houses where other customers would come to claim their goodies. It was a whole new approach with its own set of logistical considerations – not the least of which was the extra driving for us and timing of arrivals and departures. We resolved to make it a win-win for all.

Alice and I are usually fairly observant about inconveniences like the new market rules and the stressful conditions at the locker – both signals that it's time for a change. We usually look immediately for the path of least resistance and turn lemons into lemonade.

Recently we missed a flight and were forced to stay overnight in Dallas. Inconceivable! That just doesn't happen to us. We took it in stride – eventually making lemonade. Well, to tell the truth, we did everything we could think of to give back the lemons and get where we wanted to go at the time we originally wanted to be there.

After exhausting those possibilities as well as a couple of airline employees and ourselves in the upstream battle, we resigned ourselves to the unforeseen plan and said, "Okay, we're not flying anymore today. There must be a good reason." And we made the best of it.

Only a few days later did we have our "Aha!" moment when the manager at the new resort we visited confided, "It's a good thing you didn't arrive when you were scheduled to because we didn't have any place ready for you."

We got a lot of satisfaction out of remembering our fun night and fabulous meal in Dallas and were thankful for not getting to the jungle resort before we had a place to stay.

That kind of blind faith has carried us farther than we could possibly imagine or explain to most folks. I truly think it was born out of the "Isn't this just the greatest life!" proclamations that Alice would crank out as often as she could, and that I eventually adopted and embraced just as wholeheartedly as she.

Bad things just don't happen to us. Neighbor Joe O'Handlon once said, "You two could fall into the outhouse and come out smelling like roses." And we took it as the highest compliment.

We weren't smelling any roses with the meat business. We hadn't yet realized we were continuing it out of a sense of duty to our patrons, not out of a sense of joy and excitement as before. We had invested so much energy in our meat business over the past decade; we couldn't conceive that the path of least resistance might lead us completely away from it.

The glitches were highway billboards telling us that the energetic climate had shifted. We just couldn't see them. Sometimes it just takes a bigger board and a stronger whack on the side of the head. The attack on the sheep finally got our attention.

Alice and I consider ourselves the most caring stock people we know. We've converted card-carrying PETA members (People for the Ethical Treatment of Animals) to happy carnivores by our passionate efforts to raise our stock in the most comfortable, natural environment for them.

Dozens of our customers were long-time vegetarians or very occasional meat eaters relieved beyond words to find us. The animals we raised enjoyed all the best benefits of a natural lifestyle and none of the stresses:

*Daily moves onto fresh, clean pastures free of hazards.

*Small, safe herd sizes.

*Abundant sources of clean water.

*Shade and protection from the elements.

*Gentle human interactions that never invaded their flight zones. (On the contrary, we so shrank their flight zones as we gained their trust that we could touch many of our animals).

*Most importantly, protection from predators.

This last one is totally unnatural, of course. Fences, guard dogs and donkeys don't accompany the wildebeest or the caribou or the mountain sheep. Those wild beasts lead a much more stressful life than our stock.

Removing the stress on livestock is currently a huge blind spot for our country. In my mind it is no less an issue than free speech, women's right to vote, and the rights of people of color to be treated as equals.

Allan Nation, editor of the Stockman Grassfarmer magazine, advises meat marketers to NOT wear cowboy clothes to the market because a lot of urban folks will think of the Marlboro man (unhealthy smoker) and rodeo cowboys (cruelty to animals) when they see western wear. Not the best sales image.

Rodeo and other sanctioned forms of animal cruelty are on their way out and it won't come too soon. I'm talking about rodeo events like bull riding, steer wrangling, and calf roping where the animals believe they are fighting for their lives. I have the utmost respect for the events involving extreme discipline and precise communication between horse and rider.

I can't be too righteous. I'm living proof that ignorance leads to violence. In our first year of working cattle on our own, without understanding cattle and with a terribly designed working facility, I had to whack cows on the butt with a board (I thought) to get them into the work chute. At the time it seemed like the only way.

But that nightmarish experience gave us the powerful incentive to find many better ways in the following years. Even nine years later, though, in 1989, we thought we needed a dog to move sheep around. (Well, every Kiwi farmer had several – and we're grateful for the awesome companion Buckley was). But we soon had the woolies trained to come running to our "sheep, sheep, sheep" call that resulted in a brand new pasture often enough that it could call them into a stock trailer too.

Lucky never graduated into the trailer with the last class of sheep. Nor did three of the five other sheep attacked by dogs that spring. Our late-evening check on the livestock revealed a sight we'd heard about often but never before witnessed: a dog attack.

GP, our Great Pyrenees guard dog, had died several years earlier. Tight fences and Jenny the Guard Donkey, Queen Mother and Benevolent Protector of all Sheep, had continued to maintain our unblemished record. But this year we made two mistakes – fatal to three sheep and painful to many more.

We left Jenny in the paddock next to the sheep where she was helpless to defend them and we left a gap in the fence where a dog could get in. Alice had actually seen one of the dogs on our farm the day before.

We're not talking about a vicious pack of feral dogs. Playful puppies having a frolic will chase down little lambs, "pull some wool," and even give them a few bites on the butt and belly. They're not hungry or vicious; they're just excited. They get carried away and their embedded carnivore instincts take over.

We ran back to the shed in the fading light, drove the truck out, loaded five injured sheep, and set up a surgery in the shop. With artificial sinew for thread and hydrogen peroxide for sterilizing it, we stitched up layers of muscle and skin from numerous cuts on the sheep. The sheep lay still as we poked them and drew the curved needle up and out with a small pliers to make knots as we had watched the vets do countless times.

I had done a little of this before but never a solid four-hour stint of it. We worked by flashlight in the cold of the night. It was grim, silent, exhausting work — first trimming the wool around the wounds, then cutting away dirty flesh, then stitching up the muscle and skin layers the best we could — all the while trying to maintain some semblance of sterilization. It was a tiny glimpse of the horror of wartime medicine.

We saved one particular sheep for last because she'd had problems prior to the attack. Although we hadn't noticed it in the sale barn, only a few days after the flock was on our property we noticed one lamb grazing on her knees.

This in not a good sign. It usually means sore feet. Our first batch of sheep — 133 ewes bought from a single farm — ALL came down with foot rot a few days after we brought them home. It was a God-awful nightmare. The owner had told us the limpers we saw just had "mild scald" and would soon be over it. "No, it wasn't related to foot rot." We had never heard of scald. This was a big, fancy place with a thousand ewes. We were naïve.

That episode resulted in building a sheep foot bath, running them into it in lots of a dozen, and making them stand in it for 10 minutes before putting in the next group and so on till all 133 had soaked 10 minutes each. All that after putting each individual in a borrowed contraption that turned them on their side so that we could prune and trim the eaten-away parts of their tender feet.

Four feet times two toes each times 133 sheep. And repeat a few weeks later to get the parts we missed and prevent another blowup.

It was a stinky, bloody, exhausting, thankless task that called our judgment into question for ever considering adding sheep to the operation, or – at its worst – becoming farmers at all!

Kneeling sheep are a very bad sign indeed. But this one sheep would actually lie down and graze and not keep up with the flock. Plus it held its head a little low. We checked her feet, looking and smelling for the telltale rot smell. Thankfully, there was none.

What was her problem? We couldn't be sure. But she seemed to keep up so we let nature run its course, wherever that might lead. Two weeks later nature's course led to the dog attack – a terrible thing to allow and always, in my opinion, the responsibility of the sheep owners, not the dog owners. We knew how to keep dogs away but had let our defenses down.

One sheep – the one whose head hung down and didn't like to walk – was surely the slowest and easiest to catch. She was probably the first one mangled. And, speaking of natural courses, isn't that nature's perfect design for weeding out the less healthy individuals for the benefit of the community at large?

Maybe so, but this was no time for an intellectual digression on the elegance of survival of the fittest. As far as we were concerned there was no room for natural selection in our operation. We were supposed to be the final arbiter; we were supposed to choose who lived and died; we were supposed to control the timetable.

By the time we had doctored four sheep we were dead tired. We looked at the sickly sheep with the weak neck. It really wouldn't be the end of the world if that one died. It might have anyway without the attack. It now had some deep puncture wounds to the belly (which we cleaned out as best we could) as well as other wounds on her legs and rear. Perhaps she had no big skin tears like the others because she hadn't been running; she got no stitches.

We prepared a clean corner of straw in the shed and laid our wards down in it for the night. We wondered how many would be with us in the morn and collapsed into bed.

As we had feared, a closer examination of the flock in the morning light revealed more injured animals. Most injuries were slight; one was fatal. At least those in the hospital ward had all made it through the night.

It's depressing to tell this whole morbid and embarrassing story but the dog attack was an important part of Lucky's story. Obviously she lived. Just barely.

A few days after the initial shock of the attack passed, we wondered why it had happened. I don't mean we wondered why we left Jenny in the next paddock and why we hadn't patched that little hole in the low spot of the perimeter fence. I mean, "What is up with us that we would have such an experience?"

In our world, random simply doesn't exist. We see everything as interconnected and logically sequenced. The dog attack was a result of our split energy about the meat business; it was the 'big board upside the head' moment that led to serious reconsideration of the meat business. And Lucky was our reminder that we hadn't been paying attention.

# CHAPTER 14
# MORE LUCKY YEARS – PET SHEEP

L UCKY FOUGHT INFECTION with a very high fever for several days; we doubted she would live but she did. The fever blistered her skin and turned it bright pink. Her wool came out in huge patches that would puff out and drag behind her until we pulled them off. The skin underneath turned ugly colors and sloughed off, too.

She couldn't stand up on her own at all anymore so we had to help her. Plus, she sometimes got "cast," that is, stuck lying on her side, unable to get her feet under her. We made a habit of knowing where she was and checking on her hourly.

Two more of her mates died – two that we had sutured – and we expected her to give up the ghost too. The other two we doctored healed fast and we put them out with the flock, with Jenny guarding them now.

I made a pact with this sick sheep: If it wanted to go now it should show me by going over to the compost pile where I would bury it after I shot it. It hung out by the compost pile for two days! I reneged on the deal. I was a hopeless sentimental in the eyes of any stockman worth his salt.

It became apparent that this sheep wasn't ready to die so it eventually went back out with the flock. But its trials weren't over. Time and again we found it on its side – probably where it had been for hours – and helped it to its feet, but gradually that problem became less and less frequent.

Lucky's worst ordeal – yes, worse than a dog attack and high fever, I think – came when Alice and I left the farm for a weekend. We came back to notice her missing from the flock. I finally found her near a pond. She was flat on her side; the story in the soil and grass around her told me she had been that way for most of the time we had been gone.

Her down eye was full of dirt and cloudy white, maybe permanently damaged. We propped her up until her muscles could again hold her weight. She lurched around for a while but didn't fall. She took a few steps and began grazing.

She was now one-eyed, and that one a goggle eye looking up from a subservient head that flopped as she walked. Her back had a severe hump up as well as a curve to the side. She was skinny and naked but for a few ugly tufts of wool here and there. Flakes of fever-burned flesh were still peeling off. She was uglier than a baby bird, had stared death in the face three times and seemed to have an incredible will to live. We named her Lucky, obviously.

She didn't get much better. For months she couldn't stand by herself. Every time we saw her we helped her to her feet – a dozen or more times a day. From there she could decide whether she wanted to lie back down or not but she never did. It was a long time before she joined the flock again.

At harvest time we had to separate out the doctored animals from the animals headed to the butcher. But what about Lucky? If we sold her with the other doctored animals at the sale barn she would either bring the price of the others down or get sorted off and bring a dollar or two by herself. In either case her life would be more miserable than ever from that point on. After all she'd been through she didn't deserve the terror of the sale barn experience.

So at harvest time that fall there seemed only one route for Lucky and that was to stay behind. The name Lucky, once just wry sarcasm, was starting to become self-fulfilling.

By that time Lucky had strengthened to the point where she could get up by herself most of the time. Very rarely she still got stuck on her side. She stayed close to the house and shed, grazing the yard and Alice's carefully planted shrubs and flowers.

Alice had much more patience about Lucky's diet than was reasonable, in my opinion. It seemed that almost everything we had gone to a lot of trouble to purchase and plant in our landscaping plan was highly prized sheep food.

"What do you want to do about it?" she asked me.

"I don't know. We could fence the yard."

"Oh, we can't do that. We're her family now. She likes being near us."

That argument was unassailable. And it definitely seemed true that she liked being near us, though I think the word "like" is subject to wide interpretation in this case. Alice would lean toward affection whereas I would lean toward instincts, as in safety in numbers.

Whatever the case, Lucky definitely liked to get into the house whenever she could. It wouldn't be a stretch to say it was her primary goal in life. Passing unsuspectingly through the front or back door, Alice or I would suddenly be whisked into spinning pirouettes as Lucky streaked past us. Then the chase was on. But then her hooves would spin out on the slick floor after which she was easy to catch.

We lost all of our naïveté at the doors from then on. Any maneuvers requiring an open door for more than about two seconds required back-up security personnel. Since those types of maneuvers happen with some frequency (grocery bags, firewood, laundry from the line) Alice and I soon had to learn to do our own back-up security.

With arms full, it was strictly legwork. We started with all the martial arts moves we knew: no-contact side-kicks with our armload counterbalanced, threatening roundhouses as we turned the door knob, hook kicks in the air just in front of her nose – these moves would cause only a momentary pause on her part.

Next, we dropped the kicking and took up dance. Dance steps worked much better. A blocking sashay left or right, followed by a toe-tap or step-behind, was more effective but could result in a quick takedown and yard sale scattering of laundry or groceries if Lucky wasn't faked out by the block.

The cha-cha-cha and some funky, hip-hop clogging proved most effective as they combined interference with a well-known ovine gesture of hostility – the foot stomp.

Who needs a fitness center with a pet lamb like Lucky?

Despite our best efforts, Lucky did manage to break and enter on numerous occasions. Guests and kids were a pushover, so to speak. Any offense an unsuspecting guest or child might have felt at Lucky's rudeness at the door was quickly offset by the surprise and delight of watching her run through the house.

We didn't think it was at all delightful. Well, I secretly suspect Alice did like it. She always laughed hysterically as she rounded up Lucky and wrestled her out one door or the other. I was horrified and upset with the breach in training as well as the breach of the household fortress.

Actually, I have to admit it was hysterical. She seemed so pleased with herself to be inside running wild. But, on the serious side, there were three bad things that Lucky could do while in the house.

The least of the three was to eat the dog food. That's where she went first – straight toward the dog food where she would quickly stuff her cheeks like a chipmunk.

Then she'd gallop around the house looking for more adventure, knocking over anything and everything in or near her path. Chairs, tables, lamps, cats, dogs, people – she was the rampaging bull in the China shop.

Not that we have a lot of fancy things to break. We don't. But I'd rather not have any of my stuff on the floor where our four cats and dog – and sometimes sheep – walked around.

Now we're getting close to the worst of the list of inside-the-house Lucky offenses. Picture this: the front door is wide open, the groceries are strewn about on the lawn in front, and the cats are running for their lives. Buckley wants to help round up but even more wants to keep all his bones unbroken, so he stays close to the action but yelps and dodges whenever it gets too close for comfort. Alice and/or I chase and laugh (Alice) or chase and curse (you know who), and Lucky, wild-eyed, head flopping, chews and dribbles dog food, crashes into furniture, slips and dodges – struggling to get out of our grasp – and poops out a long stream of milk duds on the kitchen floor.

That's why I didn't think it was funny. Okay, she didn't do it every time. In fact she probably did it only once. But once was too much.

Sure, lamb poop cleans up easily and, heck, we've already got 20 paws and four boots tracking in God-knows-what on our floors so we're never going to win the Good Housekeeping award. But it just ain't right!

So while guests and kids are whooping with hysterics, Alice leading the chorus, I'm chuckling politely through my grimace – focused on the sole task of removing Lucky before she drops her payload. I can imagine all the laughter turning off like a switch; then a unison chorus of, "Ooooooh! Yuck!"

Needless to say, all guests meet Lucky the pet lamb right away and are told, as a casual aside, that she may try to get in the house. So you might be careful at the door. No need to get graphic and cause panic. Or disgust.

Farmers just get pretty ho-hum about crap because it is so natural. And, properly placed, it is nature's finest fertilizer. Improper placement means the shoes must come off at the door, no exceptions.

Lucky's outdoor antics are taxing enough. Her infatuation with us humans (or honorary sheep, from her viewpoint) dictates that wherever Alice and I are stopped is the current grazing ground. It is extremely endearing to be standing around anywhere within a few hundred yards of the house and have a sheep grazing contentedly six feet away. Better than a yellow, smiley, "have a nice day" balloon following you around.

That's the silver lining. The cloud is that we can't linger too long near anything we don't want Lucky to eat because she'll eat whatever is closest. She may never have shown a fondness for Miss Kim Lilac leaves and flowers but if we linger near them too long they run the risk of being denuded by Lucky.

If she were grazing on her own she'd stick to the grass; something about our focus on a plant makes her want to focus on it too! So Alice and I have to be a little sly about our landscape discussions and appreciation when Lucky is nearby, looking elsewhere to save the plants from Lucky's all-consuming appreciation. It's not easy to be loved by a sheep.

Lucky likes to sleep next to the house. To be exact, she likes to sleep against the doors. She makes the world's very best draft dodger. Trouble is, she not only blocks all the tiny spaces between the door and threshold, she also completely plugs the doggy door used by two cats and one dog.

This is unacceptable and demands a creative solution. Pulling Lucky up to standing and shoving her away was not creative enough. She would return and plop back down on the welcome mat as soon as we were out of sight.

The shoving away was most often done with a broom because ten times out of ten Lucky left a fertilizer offering on the welcome mat anyway. You should see the flowers around our porch!

Alice came up with the brilliant idea of laying a very angular piece of split firewood under the doggy door. Buck and the cats could easily step over it. Lucky, bless her heart, didn't figure out she could nudge it out of her way with her head or scrape it away with a hoof. It worked!

We almost felt guilty. Lucky had such a natural forlorn look, what with her hang-dog head and upturned eyes (yes, the bad eye did heal), that we felt like bullies to deprive her of her favorite sleeping spots. However, the need for endless sweeping finally carried the vote against her.

On our small front porch a split of firewood easily deterred Lucky. She couldn't lie on it and she couldn't avoid it and still be fully and comfortably on the porch. It had to look goofy to visitors, who might see a piece of seemingly randomly dropped firewood on the front porch as a small step from a car on cinder blocks in the front yard. We decided we could live with that.

It was the back deck that was the challenge. I had gone to a lot of trouble to make an Osage orange deck around the back door. We put a barbecue grill, picnic table, and benches out there and enjoyed the view of the pond and pasture and woods beyond. It was a favorite spot for all of us, Lucky most of all.

I'm convinced Lucky loved the new deck not only because we hung out there, but also because her tap-dancing hooves made such a satisfying percussive sound as she walked, trotted, and jumped in glee on it. Yes, jumped! The sorry little lamb had improved to the point of jumping for joy.

Maybe it was the chiropractic adjustments we gave her several times a day. Alice had asked Dr. Glenn out to adjust Luc, her thoroughbred gelding, and he did such a marvelous job – Luc's walk looked more like floating after Dr. Glenn's work – that she asked him if he could help Lucky's back.

"Oh my," chuckled Dr. Glenn as he saw a chiropractor's dream back. He ran his magic fingers along Lucky's spine, shoved down, and I swear it sounded like cracking walnuts!

We made it a habit to "adjust" Lucky every time we passed her. She seemed to like it. For whatever reason Lucky became a very happy sheep, jumping for joy when we walked out of the house, jumping for joy when it was apparent that we were going for a walk, jumping for joy when a group of people were around having a good time.

The first words out of our neighbor Patti's mouth after doing our chores for a week were, "All I want in life is a man as happy to see me as Lucky is every day!"

The firewood stick at the back door didn't prevent Lucky from liberally fertilizing all other areas of the new deck. My first chore of the morning was to drag the old broom (not the new, inside, broom) and sweep the deck. How could she possibly produce so many pellets? It was astounding. Surely she dropped some on the lawn and pasture as she grazed, but it looked like she saved them all for the deck.

That made a satisfying sound too. For a few months we thought we could train Lucky not to poop on the deck. What a joke. Every time we heard the cascade begin we jumped up from our seats and yelled, "Hey! Hey!" and waved our arms like lunatics, scaring Lucky off the deck.

Then we'd sweep and go back to business as usual and, sooner or later, so would Lucky. Our friend Burt Smith, an acclaimed animal behaviorist, says he trained a sheep to fetch and I'm sure he did. But we couldn't train Lucky to not poop on our deck.

Before we were forced to make the deck off-limits to Lucky she and my great nephew, Carter, pulled a stunt that had the four of us – his parents and Alice and me – crying with laughter.

Cousin Paul and Lynn had just arrived for a visit we had all looked forward to. Paul and I are very close as he was my only cousin as we grew up together (astounding all my Amish friends, each of whom may have fifteen to twenty aunts and uncles and hundreds of cousins!). Paul and lovely Lynn's son, Carter, was a precocious but timid four-year old.

Carter had met Lucky (and had been admonished about the door after a Lucky break-in, no doubt) and, unlike Lucky, wasn't certain that he and Lucky were destined to be friends.

We stepped out on the deck to take in the pasture view and Lucky came trotting right up, of course. This frightened Carter, the only one of us eye-to-eye with the terrible beast, and flushed him out of the safety of the human group. He ran to the edge of the deck, terrorized.

Before anyone could speak, Lucky jumped straight up in the air and then ran after him. Carter, his life at stake, ran around the picnic table to get back to us, Lucky at his heels.

This was the first time Paul and Lynn had seen Lucky's leap for joy. It was such a shocking contrast to Carter's fear that we all howled with laughter. To his credit, Carter realized immediately that he was not Lucky's lunch but, rather, a source of highest entertainment.

He took off running and squealing for the far end of the deck again, now fully in charge of the game. Lucky, for her part, ripped out her highest pronk and added a mid-air twist for effect. The crowd shrieked with delight. It was better than a fireworks display. This kept up for several more rounds around the picnic table, the last few of which Paul caught on video to be enjoyed forever more.

But poor Lucky's deck days were being counted down in sweeps of the broom. That chore was barely tolerable up to a rainy spell that produced a growth spurt of lush grass and clover. Then it was absolutely intolerable.

Now every cattleman knows better than to be directly behind a cow during the lush of new grass when the fiber content of the diet is very low. A single, throat-clearing bovine cough can cause an equal and opposite reaction that can coat the side of a pick-up truck and do unspeakable injustice to an unsuspecting human. This sort of thing doesn't happen twice. You never, ever, again put yourself in a position to allow it.

Sheep aren't quite as bad as cattle in this regard, but the integrity of their pellets diminishes to the point that there are no pellets. Sweeping becomes no longer possible. A pressure washer is best, hosing down second best. Hosing down is not an option at my house where water pressure is a function of the last time I rode the bicycle and for how long. We didn't own a pressure washer. I filled several kettles full of water and slung them on the porch and hockey-sticked the nasty stuff away with the old broom.

An electric fence went up around the deck that afternoon. It was a terrible solution, totally uncreative, but an emergency response was required. Turns out I didn't need to electrify it – Lucky wouldn't challenge it. Forlorn-looking Lucky, cast out from the thrill of the porch, watched us from the other side.

But the electric fence was a pain for Alice and me to high-step over, and it was also a barrier to Buckley and the cats, so it just couldn't last. It wasn't long before I hit upon the right solution, a way to let Buckley and the cats in while keeping Lucky out.

Our deck already had Osage Orange (we call them hedge) posts at its edge every ten or twelve feet. The posts carry hedge "beams" and, together, support an overhead arbor of grape, honey-suckle and wisteria. By placing a stout chunk of tree trunk, only one foot high, at the bottom of each post and laying more hedge poles on top of those, I made a railing that matched the overhead beams and was nose high for Lucky.

A normal sheep would have climbed up on it and jumped over. But, as I hoped, Lucky couldn't. It had no effect on the cats, and Buckley finally began passing through it too, not happy at crouching in his old age. Alice and I still had to make a small high step but we could burn the nasty broom. All in all, it was a great solution.

With porch and deck secure and Lucky as mended as she could be we settled into the normal existence of a man and a woman with a pet sheep. The main difference was that we had a sheep as well as a dog as companions wherever we went. This wasn't so unusual because even our cats, Milo and Sorghum, took fairly long walks with us.

Lucky had been with us for only a year when Buckley finally gave up the ghost at age seventeen so it was nice to have her as a companion then – even if she had no redeeming canine qualities. It's hard to imagine now that we're so comfortable with Lucky and the little things we do differently because of her, but there were several months where I actively plotted to relocate her.

Neighbor Carol Ellis was my best bet. She seriously thought about adopting Lucky and I pushed hard. She had a pet lamb of her own – a normal one – that had come from another neighbor, Royce.

"They are much happier in pairs," I suggested, deviously.

"Oh, I know, I know." She was sorely tempted.

As much joy as Carol got out of her lamb, the downside of lamb ownership grew along with her lamb until she finally, sadly, asked Royce if he'd take it back.

As I wrote that last sentence Carol called and asked me if I was watching the eclipse of the moon. I stepped outside and watched the earth's shadow slowly slide off the corner of the moon. After a few minutes and beginning to get chilled in the sharp breeze, I heard a noise and Lucky came around the house and up to me, sniffed my leg, and began grazing at my feet.

"How long do sheep live?" I've wondered a hundred times since we adopted Lucky. It really doesn't matter anymore. We're a happy family now and I hope she'll be grazing at my feet for many years to come. No matter how many years she lives, we'll be thankful for every one of them. After all, they can't help but be our Lucky years.

# Chapter 15
# Market Day – A Journal Entry

### Saturday, January 18, 2003

5:10 AM. I grab the alarm clock five minutes before it's set to go off. Can't stand that sound and glad that market days are the only days I ever set an alarm. Alice is already up and getting ready.

6:20 am. Showered, dressed, fed pets, watered Jenny (the donkey), loaded the last minute stuff in the truck, and, by the light of a big full moon not yet set in the west, we're off, five minutes late.

6:45 am. We pass Bing's in Altamont where we usually stop for hot chocolates and homemade biscuits and gravy for the road. Because of the cold (it was 8° at midnight but it warmed up to 14° by the time we left home) we were a little slower starting and a little slower getting to the bigger roads. To make up the time we skip Bing's but promise ourselves hot drinks and muffins at the market after we're already set up.

7:55 am. Roll into the City Market in good time. Less than ten venders present.

8:05 am. First customer, John Elliot, arrives while we're in the last stages of setup. We chat and give him his wife's box of soup bones. He doesn't stay long. It's chilling cold and blowing light snow. Our setup is minimal today: One six-foot table, two Styrofoam display boxes, the photo book, and brochures. No sign, no books, no magazines with our pictures on the cover.

8:20 am. Alice goes to the office to pay for today's stall ($10 during the winter, $21 the rest of the year) as well as our yearly commitment to a permanent stall ($225). The latter gives us stall #139 for every Saturday we want it. This is a new stall for us and will be a switch for customers who've come to stall #117 for six years, but we decided to go to the north side of the isle, face south, and be in the shade. Plus, it's a little closer to an electric outlet where we can plug in the two freezers on the back of our pickup.

Even though we've paid for the whole year, we'll probably go to the market less than a dozen times in 2003. But when we go, we want our customers to know right where to find us. Plus we want to be sure to have a stall available as those vendors who don't pay the big money are at the mercy of "first come, first stalled" on the really busy days (when as many as 10,000 people go through the market) and might not get a spot at all.

8:25 am. Alice returns and I head to the coffee shop for double hot chocolates, apple cinnamon cake, and a banana-nut muffin. I love this market!

9:00 am. Half-way through and only six of the seventeen customers on today's list have shown up. We're not worried; this is typical.

9:10 am. A small rash of five customers comes all at once, two of whom know each other. With only a two-hour window at the market and up to twenty or thirty customers coming, this makes our booth one of the most active sites of commerce in the market, but also a social event with friendly chatter and a lot of first-name recognition. Both are a magnet for other customers. On days when there are other customers, that is. It's so cold today, most folks are staying home. As we take care of the earliest orders, pulling the boxes or bags with names on them out of the freezers and totaling the bills, everyone has a chance to see the extra items we brought today in the display boxes.

One box has lamb chops, whole leg, boned and rolled leg, and cubes in it, the other, ground beef, ground lamb, a rack, and lamb shanks. That's all we have left. The pork is sold out (except the pork sausage, which I forgot to bring) and the last of the chickens plus the last turkey are being picked up today. In the happy atmosphere while they wait on us, most folks pick out something new to try along with the cuts they've pre-ordered.

In this way we've started dozens of folks on lamb who had never even tried it before. Many of them now say it's their favorite meat. Since lamb is the highest dollar per pound of any meat we sell and it's also the easiest to raise, we're happy about that.

9:30 am. Anne and Leah hang around and chat with us. They are both psychic healers. Anne has authored two books and her husband David is a noted chiropractor in town; he's referred dozens of patients to us. We have developed a social relationship with them.

It's warming up a little and the sun is trying to break through the clouds. Anne and Leah are ready to go and we help put their boxes in the car parked next to us (one advantage of the winter months; ordinarily they'd have to park a block or two away and come get an entry pass from us to drive through the market).

9:45 am. Divin and the others on our list show up. Divin is interesting to me because he represents a shift in our typical customer. Up until very recently we've attracted wealthy, healthy types. Our meat is not cheap. We're quite used to the bargain hunters poking, prodding, asking, "How much?" and almost running away after we reply – as if just being close is going to turn their pockets inside out. A great many of our customers are referrals. When people refer us to another they do the screening for us. They don't pass us on to someone who won't appreciate us. It is the ideal form of marketing – free, and others do the work!

Divin is all smiles and, if he weren't younger than me, I'd call him a good ol' boy. He talks about his brother's farm and moose-skin boots (warm clothing being a popular topic today). He's got a healthy Midwestern twang. As I often do if I haven't found out yet, I ask Divin, "Now, where did you find out about us again?" "Oh. On the internet."

This never happened before 2002, but over the preceding year, we had picked up half a dozen good customers who simply searched the Internet, found us, and showed up on a market day! This can be traced to all the recent publicity about grass-fed benefits. As Jo Robinson said a couple years ago, "Don't pay for advertising; it will come to you." Since that time, we've been called by – and featured in – Health magazine and Mother Earth News.

10:00 am. All in and all done. Everybody showed and we're packing up. But there's more on our schedule today. Kevin, the organic-produce grower who is rapidly branching out, has signed a five-year lease on permanent store space here in the market and today we fulfill something we've spoken to him about for a long time. Today he starts carrying our meats and making them available to market-goers daily. (The KC River Market has stalls for 300 venders under three long roofs. Ringed around this traditional market area that sees activity on Saturday, Sunday, and Wednesday are permanent shops and restaurants open every day of the week.)

We pull our truck up to Kevin's store and ask him what he wants. "I'll take everything you have left. You know how chefs are – if it's in stock they'll take it." Kevin has been supplying chefs for many years and hustles all over the city. We're very happy to empty out our freezers entirely (always the goal). Besides the leftover ground beef and lamb are two orders from folks who told us they couldn't make it today. We tell Kevin to take full price for them and we sell them to him at his discount. A nice way to start our relationship and we're all very upbeat.

This isn't our first store. It's our seventh. We don't actively seek stores, but we're excited about what Kevin is starting. Of the other six, only two still carry us. And they only carry ground beef. Our other cuts usually sell out to regular customers and, frankly, we prefer the interaction with our market customers (and even our mail-order customers). Stores and restaurants are impersonal and not committed to growers. I know of one grower who was quickly pulled under when a huge restaurant account went belly up and left him holding 3000 chickens! Talk about all your eggs in one basket! What a disaster!

The best thing about having a store that carries our meat is that it's exactly like third-party certification. When we tell a new customer that they can also find our products in Wild Oats on Main or Fresh Air Fare in St. Joe, it's as if a big stamp comes out of the sky and block-prints "APPROVED" all over us. Of course, we'd rather they do the research on us – look at our pictures, ask us questions, hear testimonials from other folks – but, like the auctioneers say, "It don't matter where we start, it's where we wind up that counts."

11:15 am. We say our goodbyes and good lucks to Kevin, park the truck back in our spot and join our friends Ken and Andy who have driven to the market to join us for a brunch date. The food and atmosphere at the deli only two blocks away are pure inner city-hip and we enjoy the punk styles and "modern" food – a big change from Jamesport.

11: 40 am. Soup and sandwiches down the hatch and sharing Toblerone chocolates for dessert. Then, Ken and Andy ask if we'll be best man and maid of honor at their wedding this fall! Of course, we say, shocked and honored. They excitedly discuss the wedding plans.

12:15 pm. We say good-byes to Andy and Ken and head for our last stop – Wild Oats.

12:25 pm. Deliver 30 lbs. of ground beef to our favorite store and do some shopping for fruits and vegetables. We've been in this store since 1995, saw it purchased by Wild Oats, and then watched Wild Oats become more and more corporate. The latest burden for small producers is UPC codes on all labels. Since Wild Oats represents a tiny fraction of our business we won't incur the time and expense to do that if and when they force it upon us. Ah well, to everything there is a season.

12:40 pm. On our way home after a great market day. Alice does the traditional "counting of the loot." I'm very keen that it be respectable if not impressive since I had already decided to make this day public in a journal. "$2020," she announces. That's respectable. We've done much better before, but that's probably not far from an average market day.

I have quipped before that I make $1000 an hour selling meat and this is how. Of course, that's just the selling of it. The preparation takes much more time...but that's a story for another day.

# Chapter 16
# Community Development

I T HELPS TO see one's world through another's eyes every now and
then.

As I said goodbye to Eyob and Fai, two students from my alma mater,
Grinnell College, who had just spent a week with me as externs studying
sustainable agriculture, sustainable living, and sustainable community
development, I had a new appreciation for my Jamesport community.

Both first year students, Eyob was born in Sudan, the son of refugees from
the war-torn Republic of Eritrea, and Fai was a resident of Thailand and
the daughter of college professors. We spent the week visiting friends and
neighbors in Jamesport -- both Amish and not -- engaging in stimulating
conversations ranging from the physics of information to interpretations
of theories of community development.

The theories of development caught my interest immediately as they mirror
the polarity of current agricultural thoughts. The interpretations fall under
the broad titles of modernization and dependency, with differing ideas
on how to solve the problems of so-called undeveloped countries. One
believes in modernization through technology and the other believes that
technological infusion only leads to dependency.

The assumption behind modernization that "undeveloped countries need
bolstering" reminds me of Stan Parson's famous line, "If technology is the
solution to agriculture, what's the problem?" It is the inappropriate use of
technology – from the plow to genetic manipulation – that wreaks the most
havoc on our planet. From desertification to unprecedented flooding, from

salmonella outbreaks to rampant obesity from nutrient-deficient food, the culprit is most often the inappropriate application of technology.

The modernists support the corporate model of development: economically driven and government supported, with corporate interests dominating individual interests and with little to no regard for the impact on local cultures. The modernists see the transfer of technology on a global level as the answer to development problems. Whether economic stimulation is the goal or the result of this policy depends on one's level of skepticism. In my opinion, only the very naïve can believe policies that force open markets are altruistic.

Dependency theorists look deeper into the social implications of technological transfer across cultures. They note the undermining of cultures (particularly AGRI-cultures) when cheap, foreign products (food, for example) become available. Traditional ways and traditional foods are dropped in favor of the easy, cheap, and new. As a result, developing countries become dependent on those that supply them, suffer from an erosion of culture, and acquire a whole new set of problems to deal with.

It puts me in mind of the saying, I think attributed to President Harry Truman, "If you want to make a man a cripple, give him crutches."

To those of us flirting with, or deeply engaged in, alternative agriculture, these are familiar poles of thought. Can there be a global industry more polarized than agriculture? On one end are the front-page, glitzy, scientific triumphs: gene-spliced tomatoes, Roundup-ready soybeans, and cloned calves that accomplish … what?

An inedible tomato, a soybean guaranteed to make you buy herbicides, and five expensive sources of hamburger. Yes, I admit it's cool that we can do those things. But just because we can doesn't mean we should.

And on the other end, without fanfare, are naturalist farmers who mimic time-tested patterns of nature to grow healthy, tasty, food while building organic matter and healthy soil.

As Fai and Eyob and I toured Jamesport and spoke to Amish and "English" friends, we dove deeper into the subject of appropriate development. Our first stop was at my neighbor Joe Burkholder's new store, Oak Ridge Furniture. Joe recently built a giant store with a show room, workshop, and storage areas and moved his young family to a house nearby.

Joe is twenty-five, handsome, and self-assured beyond his years. He is quick to smile and disarming with stories of his blunders and near-blunders. How was it that he built this business, had so much inventory, employees (actually more like sub-contractors), and responsibility at an age barely more than a college graduate?

This was a question that I hadn't heard Joe asked before and the answer was insightful. Like all Amish boys, Joe worked outside of the home after his school years were over and some of that time was in a furniture shop. At the age of seventeen he fell in love with the furniture business and that began a dream of a business of his own.

"I believe if you have a goal and work hard you can achieve it," Joe said.

I was mightily impressed with all three of these youngsters – all conversing in their second language. I knew I was in for a good week.

Several times later in the week we visited my good friend and right arm, Abe Kurtz. At only twenty-six, Abe has a home with his wife, Susie, and three daughters on 160 of the best acres near Jamesport; a growing herd of cattle; and a large shop housing a thriving tarp business as well as our new mini-assembly line for poultry-processing equipment. Abe has as much confidence and humility as you can stuff inside one young man.

There were no surprises with Abe's answers until a later visit when I tested my budding theory that tied technology and freedom together. It went like this:

Modern folks, certainly governments and corporations, see development as primarily education and technology transfer with maximum commerce involved. It is really commerce driving it, but we can give the powers that be – politicians, bureaucrats, and CEOs – the benefit of the doubt and say that they truly have the best interests of humanity at heart. I'm sure many of them do.

This is the prevailing model that is meddling with countries like Eyob's and Fai's to help "raise their standards of living." Well, are they really helping?

The long answer is yes and no and roughly parallels the plusses and minuses of the large corporate hog farms that moved into north Missouri recently. On the positive side, the confined animal feeding operations, CAFOs as they call themselves, provide jobs and an increased tax base. On the minus, they pollute and squeeze out the little producers. That is a gross simplification. And the ramifications of development on a global scale are much more complex to sort out.

There is no black and white. Development comes in shades of grey and looks different from each individual perspective. So how, then, can a person make any type of objective qualitative judgment as to whether a form of development is good or bad?

I was at a loss. Then I fell back on the premise that carried Alice and me out of the dark years of farming back in the 80s, the four words that became our farm motto: nature is the model. I fell back on my training in biology and the unassailable truths of nature. If we looked at models of development through the lens of nature's template it is easy to see where they clash with nature. We can, therefore, easily sort out the appropriate from the inappropriate.

With the naturalist's glasses on, most of the clashes are obvious and severe: Confinement, manure aggregation, and concentrated rations of primarily corn and soybeans, though all currently considered "best management practices" by our highest authorities – government agencies and land-grant universities – cannot be found in any natural systems. And therefore each one is a risky proposition requiring a lot of technological props. They are doomed to failure because Mother Nature always bats last. What doesn't work becomes extinct.

Exporting cheap foods, machinery for automated production, and western technology also flies in the face of natural development. It causes cultural upheaval and radical changes in diet and nutrition. The Western world can't seem to look outside its borders without feeling that every family ought to have two cars, three TVs, and medical benefits.

After considering biology and nature's example of sustainable development, Fai and Eyob and I came back to looking at the Amish. How do they stack up? Of course, they fail miserably by typical standards: not enough education, lower income, poorer access to medicine (no insurance, no phones for emergencies). By modern measures of success - cars and televisions - they aren't even on the radar screen.

The western mind sees Amish and sees what they don't have: vehicles, televisions, computers, fashionable clothes. Looking at them through nature's checklist for sustainable development, however, they get an amazingly high report card.

* They accept no government assistance. (Yet still they have to pay taxes.)

* They contribute hardly at all to air pollution and energy consumption.

* They trade locally, stimulating the local economy (unlike corporations that out-source all over the world).

* They invest locally. All their earnings stay right at home. They invest in land, more buildings, and CDs in the local bank.

* They produce most of their own food from their huge gardens and the livestock they grow. Very little of their food has been trucked from afar.

* They are better land and animal stewards. There are exceptions here, but on the whole they keep more soil on the land and take better care of their stock than their "English" counterparts.

* They use manures instead of formulated fertilizers. Again there are exceptions, but many have dairies and spread cow and horse manure on crop fields.

As significant as all those high marks are, they pale in comparison to the big realization I had about the Amish when we had our second discussion with Abe: Could they be freer because of their shunning of technology?

Look at the Western world's approach and results: We are handing out crutches left and right and making cripples of the poor both in our nation and in developing countries. We are taxing ourselves heavily and subsidizing global corporate greed – all in our quest to hand out more crutches. Look at our obese population. Look at the skyrocketing number of non-ambulatory people. We have arrived at a fascinating and precarious stage in population growth and health through our accepted western model of development.

But look at the Amish. With eighth-grade educations and a long arm's length from the government, they are producing young men like Joe and Abe: entrepreneurs who add value to their local economies and raise healthy, well-adjusted children who will have a sense of responsibility to the family, a sense of contribution, a practical view of the world, and priorities that revolve around community strength.

In front of Eyob and Fai, I asked Abe if he ever felt like he had been deprived in any way by being raised Amish. Almost bashfully Abe said, "I really feel like I had more freedom being raised Amish."

That's when the truck of truth hit me. Of course! It's the community safety net, the family values, the personal freedom, and the responsibility that make for individual strength and security. What "English" twenty-five year olds did I know who shouldered half the responsibility of Abe or Joe? None. I certainly didn't at twenty-five.

It makes sense when you see eight- and ten-year old boys and girls driving a team of horses in the hay field, doing exactly the same amount of work as their older siblings and father and uncles. It makes even more sense when you understand that any money earned before the child comes of age – usually twenty-one – goes to the family and, in turn, when the child marries or comes of age, the parents help set them up on property of their own.

Working for Mom and Dad is not at all objectionable when you know that, down the line, Mom and Dad's economic well-being is going to have a big impact on how well you get established when you leave the nest.

It is a system that maximizes personal responsibility. And, following that, what can be more freeing than knowing your own capabilities, having the confidence to strike out on your own, and to set and strive for your own goals? They are freer because they have found out who they are at an earlier age!

So many children today are coddled and sheltered and, consequently, inept when Mom decides they need to get out on their own. I rarely see Amish parents mother-henning their kids. The kids play at games that many of my friends would consider high risk. And sure, there are tears, cuts, scrapes, and minor accidents.

Abe related a telling story. Some Amish women noticed from inside the house two very little boys climbing up the ladder of a tall silo. The women were very worried but just watched from inside as the boys went all the way up, poked around, and then climbed back down. Abe said the women knew if they had gone outside and called to the boys, the boys would have known that their mothers and aunts were afraid for them. That in turn could have made the boys feel fearful about what they were doing. The women put their desire to have the boys growing up confident and unafraid before their maternal instincts to fear for their safety. It takes wisdom and discipline to allow children that kind of freedom and experiential learning.

Who is going to be a more functional global citizen, a child who understands through experience how the world works and where his or her limitations lay, or one who is scared to go outside where he or she might get stung or scratched or dirty?

I'm convinced, despite the strict dress code, despite the horse and buggy, despite the limited travel and exposure to the world, and most of all, because of their shunning of technology and their ideas on parenting, the Amish are, as a whole, freer than the "English" and epitomize the best model of appropriate development: the empowerment of the individual.

*David Schafer*

Any reasonable plan for community development, be it within one's own country or for export to a developing country, would do well to consider that countries are composed of communities and communities are composed of individuals. Empowered individuals are the true backbone of sustainable communities and strong countries.

It does my heart good to see, through my vantage point of poultry equipment sales, the emergence of a new breed of courageous and optimistic folks, young and old, Amish and not. Allan Nation of the Stockman Grass Farmer has called them the farmers of tomorrow. I like to think of them as rural entrepreneurs, modern pioneers, and risk-takers who see the bigger picture, who carefully choose their technological tools, who hold on to a land ethic that precludes plundering, and who have at heart a basic understanding of nature's model and scale.

These folks are more self-reliant, have old-fashioned values, are more optimistic, family-oriented, nature-oriented, and more spiritual in traditional and non-traditional ways.

I want to thank Fai and Eyob, fellow Grinnell Pioneers, for opening my eyes to these insights and making me thankful, once again, for my community, my values, and my service.

Thanks Fai, thanks Eyob. The new world belongs to your generation. May your memories of Jamesport serve you well.

# CHAPTER 17
# PASTURED POULTRY - SOCIAL ACTIVISM

YESTERDAY A FELLOW drove a 12-hour round trip to pick up his poultry-processing equipment. I couldn't meet him so I made arrangements for him to meet with Abe, the twenty-five-year-old Amish man who does the lion's share of our equipment assembly and knows as much about it as anybody. I dropped by Abe's later that evening to pick up the check and see how it went.

The long list on the receipt book was pleasing to both of us but Abe had a bigger story to tell. The two spent an hour and a half together, including some time in Abe's house where Abe showed him one of the carts we offer for sale as work tables.

Abe first found the cart as a present for his wife, Susie. It was a multi-purpose storage cupboard, transport vehicle, serving station, counter space, and, not least of all, a sometimes play station for their three little girls, all under school age. A multi-tasking tool for a multi-tasking wife, in other words.

"He took one look at it and that was enough," Abe said smiling.

We were both happy that Abe's idea for a companion to the equipment we manufacture was a hit. I'm guessing something about Abe's sincerity and deep satisfaction with life touched our new customer because he opened up to Abe.

"He told me something kind of funny," Abe said. "He said several years ago he didn't have a reason to live."

Abe brought his thumb and forefinger an inch apart. "He said he was this close to being dead."

Three years ago, Abe thought assembling our equipment was a great supplement to his tarp shop business; it could allow him to work at home full time with his family. Since then, the allure of pastured poultry seems to have rubbed off on him and he has a greater appreciation for the business. He asked to read my Salatin books. Then we took in the thrill of a Joel Salatin talk together in Bloomfield, Iowa in a room packed with over 300 other Amish.

Abe is as quick as they come and rapidly assimilated Joel's production, processing, and marketing philosophies. In fact, he even got the "worldly view" of Joel through a television set in one of the universe's most perfectly orchestrated, serendipitous moments.

As the meeting finished, Abe and Susie and I decided on a place to grab dinner with Joel and his hosts before we drove our separate ways. About ten of us met at Joe's Diner in Bloomfield. At first I wondered how, in all of Bloomfield, we had picked this little dive. Oh well, the company would make up for any shortfalls in food or atmosphere. We placed our orders at the counter and moved toward the largest table. But before we could sit down somebody said, "Look at that!"

Our eyes followed the outstretched arm and finger toward an overhead TV set that showed Michael Pollan talking on the nightly news! Michael Pollan, author of "The Omnivore's Dilemma," the bestseller that broke the pasture-raised farming story across the nation.

In telling that story, Pollan tells Joel's story, of course. And Pollan is a wordsmith in a class of his own. If you are reading this, you'd love Omnivore's Dilemma.

It was easy to guess the general topic of the news report without being able to hear the interview – food choices in America. Probably another salmonella outbreak somewhere. Then, sure enough, they cut from the Pollan interview to clips of Joel's farm!

We whooped and dropped our jaws all at the same time. What are the odds of the split-second timing? Of all the TV my Amish friends have been exposed to in their lives – probably amounting to very few hours –what are the odds that they'd catch this?!

In shock, I asked Joel, "How many times has your farm been on national news?"

"Only once that I know of," he responded, equally incredulous.

Both Abe and Susie shared that magic moment and came home sprinkled with fairy dust like folks always do after a Joel talk. I was pretty sure our new customer had been sprinkled, too, and Abe agreed.

How cool is it that we are in a business to support an endeavor that is literally life giving? Without words, Abe and I shared the satisfaction of that thought.

That has given me pause to reflect: Why is it so life giving?

What makes the endeavor of raising our own poultry on pasture so special? It isn't just about Joel's charisma, is it? Certainly he has the passion of a thousand but that's getting the cart before the horse.

Joel's passion stems from the leading-edge cause that he pioneered and of which he will always be the reigning champion (until, perhaps, his son, Daniel, accepts the title). He would be happy if more were out there championing the cause with him, but few have the eloquence, and none have the history to be another Joel.

But anyone who takes up the mantle of a pastoralist, whether it be with chickens or cattle or hogs or sheep, steps out of the conventional mold and steps into a leading-edge, exciting, society-reforming vocation.

Yes, social reformation. Social activism, if you'd prefer. That action, just that decision alone – to raise the poultry or whatever in a more natural way – puts us firmly in the camp of Those who care for the land, Those who care for the animals, Those who care for pure food, Those who care for our society at large.

That's powerful! But there's more. That decision also tells the world, "I choose my own path." How freeing is that? No government guide sheets to follow, no corporate sponsors. Only us, nature's template, the canvas of our farmland, and our supportive customers.

And there's the final, highest, and the least expected reward: Customer appreciation!

Pastured poultry raisers are champions, modern day Robin Hoods, to their urban counterparts. We save their families from salmonella, bird flu, e coli, polluted lakes and streams. We liberate them from the disturbing thought of supporting crowded, factory farms with their ammoniated atmospheres and fecal dust-covered everything. We replace their vision of chicken hell with chicken heaven.

Many urbanites, exposed to more media, and certainly more removed from food self-sufficiency than their rural cousins, are scared to death of their food, and are desperate for healthy alternatives. Food safety is absolutely fundamental; it trumps all other issues. This is the stirring sense one gets from hearing Joel speak. There is no higher calling. We are freedom fighters for safe food and heroes and heroines to eaters, animals, and ecosystems everywhere.

Doesn't this role put us on the front lines of social activism? It's like refusing to sit in the back of the bus. Reaching back further, it's like the women's suffrage movement, like the termination of slave holding, like the Boston Tea Party!

Yes, it is a bold act of revolt against the current food paradigm. In a food environment that is corporate-dominated, heavily subsidized, government hog-tied, ultra-processed, and walled off from public scrutiny, how daring is it to be a one-man or one-family operation, totally transparent, without a subsidy "safety net," producing food as pure as snow, selling out of our own backyard? In America today – that's daring. And desperately needed.

It is a dignified act of revolt in the Gandhi vein, and not at all unlike the Amish shunning of modern ways. We are not getting in anyone's face about the circus of calamities of modern food production. We are humbly stepping up to the task of showing the world how to do the job in a better way.

As in any leading-edge movement, there are obstacles to overcome. Local authorities – the meat inspectors – have mistakenly told countless poultry producers that they can't do what they're doing. The prepared poultry enthusiast will direct them to Public Law 90-492 that exempts from government inspection anyone raising up to 1000 poultry. (Inspectors may not like to be surprised with this information, so deliver it as gently as possible.)

Back in 1989, our first inspector, Louie, said, "I'm not inspecting no damn sheep!" We stared back with big lamb eyes and said, "But you have to." And he did have to. The point is that those folks aren't used to not calling the shots. Tread lightly around their egos; you may need their help some day.

The thing about inspectors is – they don't have to know we exist if we stay small. They'd rather not know, believe me. As soon as they know, they are obligated to have jurisdiction over our operations and make sure we stay within the parameters of the law.

I say, "Embrace your social activism," whether it be as a farmer or as a conscientious eater. Be proud to lead the change for the better. Be proud to assume control of one small segment of the food supply. Have pride in better products, better land, and better care of animals. Enjoy the ride on the leading edge. After all, only the lead dog gets the view.

And, finally, knowing too well how skeptics think (being a card-carrying one myself), I would say the following to anyone who has come this far with me and decided, "Oh, he's just trying to sell more equipment."

Alice and I raised and sold pastured poultry for six years before we even thought about manufacturing equipment. We know the empowering feeling of doing what is right for the land, livestock and our customers, friends and family. It is that conviction that drives my passion for the poultry equipment business, not the other way around.

The equipment sells itself because it supports a deeply freeing reason to live with passion: being a part of social reform.

# Chapter 18
# Chicken Plucker Factory

Abe was in control from the moment he came to me to say he'd like to be in line to make chicken pluckers.

I'd never given it a thought but I did now, listening to him. The family pallet shop where Abe, the eldest son, had basically been foreman since he was fourteen held no long-term appeal to Abe. He was good at it and knew how to make money at it. But even before marrying Susie Schrock, Abe was looking for a way to work from home and be near his future wife and family. This was the first of many times I found Abe looking further out into the future than I was.

I need people like that around me. Alice is a planner par excellence, which is a source of joy and frustration to us because we are so unlike each other but such good teammates. I'm a card-carrying creative, playing with the most fun thought of the moment, hopelessly lost without my to-do list. Alice is a linear-thinking, task-oriented doer.

We had recently shifted our small base of chicken-plucker operations from Syl's to Carl Miller's just up the road from Syl. Syl Graber suggested Carl as his replacement when Syl and his four boys decided to buy the sawmill of Abe's uncle, Andy Kurtz, and work there full time. No, Andy wasn't going to take over for Carl to complete the neighborhood circle, but the circle of commerce within an Amish community is almost that tight.

The Amish man - those similar to my Jamesport neighbors anyway - is the ultimate entrepreneur. First of all, he's a farmer to some degree. At the very least he has a horse pasture, some hay land and a barn. It is likely he grows oats to harvest along with the hay. Then he may have a conventional cash crop like corn or soybeans or wheat. Or an unconventional cash crop like pumpkins, onions, or melons. He may have a greenhouse or two to grow tomatoes or flowers. He's probably got some laying hens. A handful in Jamesport raise pastured poultry – chickens and turkeys - for meat. He may have a milk cow or dairy goats. One here has a large herd of meat goats. There are a few pig operations, farrow to finish, that is, from birth to market. Quite a few have small dairies. Many have beef cow herds. Nearly a dozen in Jamesport raise deer. Several raise horses and mules commercially. The average Amish farm around Jamesport has less than 200 acres and supports eight or ten people. The average non-Amish farmer around here farms closer to 1000 acres though he may own only half of those. Those 1000 acres of land support four or five people.

The Amish can support so many people because they have so much available labor. It's a circle fueled by their creativity and procreativity. As large as the list of farming enterprises appears, the cottage industries run out of the house, basement, or shop outbuilding surpass that number.

A steady stream of furniture of all types flows out of Jamesport. Playground equipment, outdoor furniture, cabinets, cedar chests, rustic cedar furniture, distressed furniture, dining-room tables and chairs, bureaus, dressers, the list is endless. There are four sawmills that feed as many pallet shops.

In addition to all the woodworkers there are metal shops and small-engine repair shops and metal suppliers. Plus plumbing suppliers, general farm-goods suppliers, fence suppliers, chimney suppliers, stove dealers, candy makers, bread bakers, quilters, sewers, tarp shops, harness shops, buggy-repair shops, wheelwrights, lumber suppliers, shoe shops, farriers (horseshoers), grain-ration mixers, garden supplies. Oh dear, who have I missed?

There are dealerships galore. There are dealers of animal supplements – feeds, vitamins, health enhancers; human supplements – tonics, more vitamins, oils; and garden products – seeds, sprays, fertilizers. There are dealers of chain saws, mowers, massage equipment, bird houses, you name it. Basically, if it's used among the Amish, someone (or two) probably has a dealership in order to bring in the best prices and add another income stream to the family operation.

Just the labor specialties are staggering. There are crews proficient in any aspect of building that doesn't use a lot of heavy equipment:. Cement, framing, roofing, stonework, brickwork, drywall, paint, flooring, siding and gutters, plumbing, and even electricity. There are several who are full-time horse or mule trainers.

The typical non-Amish farm has three or four enterprises: corn, soybeans, maybe wheat, maybe cattle, and always the government commodity-program subsidy check. The typical Amish farm may have a dozen enterprises: eggs, quilts, garden produce, two or three or four types of livestock, two or three cottage businesses, a cash crop or two, perhaps some teenage boys or girls who hire out (their wages go back to the family), and sometimes the head of the family works out, too. Sawing logs, selling firewood, making butter or jam, and even rabbits also contribute.

I don't think we realized it at the time when Alice and I gravitated eight miles down the road to Jamesport but I now believe we were seeking community. Just living around such diversity and creativity has rich benefits and conveniences that cannot be found elsewhere. More people are around, especially young, energetic people. The fields are smaller – human scale, we call them – and aesthetically pleasing. There is an abundance of fresh produce and farm-raised meat and dairy products. Also, a large and willing labor pool is at hand.

Abe was willing to convert part of an old dairy barn on his farm into a dedicated work space to build chicken pluckers. He had seen firsthand my first big commercial step into the world of chicken pluckers when his family made fifty-five odd-sized pallets for shipping my "Featherman Jr." chicken pluckers, which had been imported from Indonesia. We had gotten to know each other a little during my trips to his shop to pick up a handful of pallets at a time.

I've always believed in wearing a belt and suspenders too, so to speak. I don't always practice it but I believe it. Abe's farm was closer to me and I was uncertain about how fast we were going to grow in our first years of production. So far, production had always been behind orders. But because Carl Miller also had a window business and was mostly looking to fill in his slow winter months with work for me, I felt that adding another production line with Abe seemed like good insurance to keep my pants from falling down, so to speak.

Right away I noticed that Abe was different from the rest of us. I'm generous to include myself with Syl and Carl because, although I didn't assemble the first fifty-five imported pluckers from scratch, I had to wire and install motors and pulleys and switches on them. After those imports were all sold and we began our own manufacturing, it was Syl who put the chicken pluckers together out of his farm shop.

Syl and Carl and I are a lot alike. Our organizational skills are about average or a little above. But Abe was in a category of his own.

Even though his first "shop" was a dusty, old, eight-stall dairy parlor that hadn't seen use for quite a few seasons, he had it cleaned up and laid out like a banquet table for the queen. Whether this was a carry-over from his pallet-shop habits, an attempt to compensate for the world's sorriest shop in all other respects, or just a reflection of Abe's personality I wasn't sure at first. In any case, I was impressed.

Abe always built five pluckers at a time. He first gathered the parts and put them on the cow's-butt side of the stalls. On his own he purchased a rolling worktable with many compartments in which he stored all the little parts as well as the tools. This rolling parts/tools station moved up and down the line with him. Medium-sized parts he pulled out of the mangers on the other side of the head catches. Packaging, wire scraps, plastic trim, and miscellaneous trash went in to the poop gutter where it was easily swept up and disposed.

It was quite entertaining and educational to watch. As he worked, Abe found one way after another to save time and increase the consistency of the product. He surprised me by purchasing expensive tools. But he had done the math and knew how much time they saved and how soon they would pay for themselves. He was being paid by the piece and I watched as his hourly return rose higher and higher.

"Hey! This isn't fair. I'm paying you too much!" It was tempting to say, but I always managed to resist that temptation and replace it with admiration. Abe earned every penny.

Prior to Abe, one of our biggest problems was getting behind on orders. With Abe on board, even though he only worked when he was off from the pallet shop, being behind was history. He took the pressure off Carl and me both.

Abe and I started a recurring conversation about having him work full time. It was an exciting idea for both of us. It was his goal to work out of his home. Could I guarantee him enough work?

That answer put me walking on a high wire. I loved the idea of a bright young man like Abe being able to reach for a dream of his by helping me reach for a dream of mine. But guarantee? How could I tell what was going to happen with orders? Plus, I couldn't just pull the rug out from under Carl.

Abe didn't expect me to cut Carl off. Carl is Abe's uncle. Esther, Carl's wife, is younger sister to Mary, Abe's Mom. They are family.

I honestly don't know how the Amish keep track of all their kin. I grew up with one first cousin. They each have hundreds. Their reunions are more like conventions. One young Amish man said, "I went to a reunion and met myself!"

When you've been around here long enough you recognize a new face as belonging to a certain family.

"You must be a Schrock."

"That's right."

"Would that be Robert's side or Leroy's?"

No fooling. We were eating lunch one day with our good friend Kenny King and his son Daniel in Hutchison, Kansas, and I knew the Amish fellow at the next table had to be related to some of our Schrocks. One of the Amish boys that had come with us to see Kenny's pioneering farm store with their own meat and dairy products was Jacob Schrock. He introduced himself after the meal and it turned out this gentleman was a brother to Robert and Leroy.

Kenny, just to digress briefly, played a very important role in the home poultry-processing evolution/revolution. He visited us way back in the mid-90s just after Ernie Kauffman, our Amish friend with a butcher shop, had cobbled together the first homemade plucker out of a lawn mower engine and a sawn-off plastic tub.

Kenny was the first to commercialize the tub plucker in his "Jako" line of equipment. It was brilliant and cut the entry costs in half. It would be almost five years later before I imported what would become the Featherman Jr. to sell at less than half the price of Kenny's plucker. Well, I had to do it. Folks needed the economy. Kenny forgave me.

I wanted to encourage Abe's entrepreneurial spirit but I didn't want to get him out on a limb that wouldn't support him. We had gone to a more professional model by then – a molded plastic base and tub rather than a welded base and the sawn-off plastic barrel – and several hatcheries had discovered us.

McMurray Hatchery in Webster City, Iowa was a huge breakthrough for us. Syl and I visited them to show our contraption. They were impressed but said it needed to look more professional. Was there a demand? McMurray didn't offer any tub pluckers because they were all way too expensive ($4000) for the Mom and Pop operations. The previous year they had sold 27 table-top pluckers which require the operator to hold the bird and press it against rotating rubber fingers. Those went for $795 plus shipping and had to be assembled. For $200 more, wouldn't people want a plucker that operated automatically and could do four chickens at a time right off the delivery truck?

That was our gamble when we approached Bill Coon at his plastic fabrication plant and spent a small fortune to make our molds. Bill, a farmer, and Troy, his welder and an old friend of mine, spent a lot of time with us on the design. McMurray's customers liked what we came up with and we were off and running.

How fast and far we were going to run was what Abe was asking. I kept my answers encouraging but non-committal.

One day Abe put a chill through me when he informed me he was quitting the pallet shop. He had acquired a tarp shop business from his uncle Paul. (It was Uncle Andy, Uncle Paul's brother, who sold the sawmill to Syl, and Uncle Carl, Aunt Esther's husband, in the other plucker shop, who took over from Syl when Syl bought Uncle Andy's sawmill. Are you keeping up?)

"Have you penciled it all out?" I asked.

"I think so. But you've got to keep the plucker orders coming!" Abe's left eye winked rapidly like a bug had flown in to it.

I was all smiles for his opportunity, his courage, and our budding business. As it was going, Carl was very busy with his window business and Abe was building the lion's share of pluckers.

But quitting the pallet shop and moving home wasn't Abe's last, or biggest, leap of faith. His little dairy parlor was free for the dusting, close to the house, and easy to heat. (Tight, in other words.) He had a limited amount of inventory storage space there.

One morning Abe presented me with plans for his new shop, a 40x80-foot monster. I knew what it cost to build metal buildings and pour 3200 square feet of concrete. My jaw dropped as my head and shoulders backed away from him.

"Are you serious?" We both stared at the plans.

"The front half will be half tarp shop and half plucker shop and the back half will be inventory storage. A wall with a garage door will divide them in two. And there will be a bathroom here."

I couldn't believe it.

"And you'll like this," he looked up at me. "We'll have three loading docks. Customer pick-up, Fedex and UPS truck, and motor freight."

Accommodating these three different truck heights had been a challenge for us.

"The way I see it," Abe explained, "I've committed to this business and to keep the work here on my farm, I need a facility that can handle our growth for several years to come."

And that's exactly what he built. On his own. Without a nickel from me. See what I mean about way out in front of me?

Carl Miller built a new shop too, one in which he and his boys could actually make the windows he sold and installed. That covered his family full time, so the timing was just right to shift all the plucker-building business over to Abe.

One thing about that new shop really bothered me, though. Even though I hadn't put a nickel into the darn thing it was full of my stuff and Abe would not give me a key to it.

"Why not?" I asked. "What if I need to get something for someone?"

"I'm almost always around, for starts," he grabbed his index finger. "And if it's on a Sunday, they don't need it." He paused patiently holding two fingers. "And if I happen to be gone, Vernon's (Susie's brother and his family up the road) have a key you can borrow." Three strikes and I was out of rebuttals.

As usual, he had anticipated my response and rehearsed his. Creative types cannot win arguments against the logical types, I knew from marital experience. I threw my hands up in the air and walked away.

"I've got half my life savings in your shed and I can't have a key!" I said loudly to the sky.

Abe shouted back his final – surely rehearsed – volley, "The business is safer this way!" I could hear him laughing.

Dang. He was right. I had to laugh, too.

Remember the Green Hornet TV series of the 60s? His Asian sidekick/ martial arts expert would keep him sharp by hiding and ambushing him? That started happening in the shop with Abe and me. He'd hear me drive up and hide behind the trash bin, hide behind the file cabinet, hide behind a load of merchandise on the dock, then leap out with a "WHAAH!"

Sometimes after creeping around in a crouch for three minutes, I had to come to the conclusion he wasn't there. But if I saw him leaving the house I had 30 seconds to hide on my own. Of course, with my vehicle parked at the shop there was no doubt I was there so he'd act extra casual as he came in and not bat an eye when I showered him with plastic curls I'd gathered from the floor.

Yes, it was strictly a business relationship, all seriousness. Abe was happy as a lark in his new home shop. It was spacious, light, warm, and had plenty of room for the kids to play. Within a few days of setting up shop and settling in, Abe's standard greeting – when he wasn't ambushing me – was to call out, "Chicken Plucker Factoreeeee!" in a high falsetto.

So far in five years the greeting hasn't lost its humor. We are both in love with his shop.

As much as we are, it may be Susie, Abe's frau, who appreciates it the most. When the shop was built, only Beth and Susannah were on the scene and they were great shop helpers. The little rubber fingers of our pluckers were particularly good play toys and some would actually get poked into the holes Abe drilled. More often they were spread out over the large shop floor while Daddy worked nearby.

The advantages to Mom and Dad and family were the best side results any business could have. Then along came Rachel Ann and there were three girls. The 'girlies.' Rachel Ann is my baby. I claim her because I anguished through her birth just like a parent would.

Abe asked me if I wanted to be the driver on call when the next baby came around. In a moment of weakness I said yes. I've been very careful to remain off the driver call lists that wallpaper the Amish phone boxes.

I feel the non-Amish folks living among our Amish community are delighted to have their Amish friends and all of them have favorites. It's a two way street and it is especially nice for an Amish person to have a car-driving "English" friend who saves him $15 or $20 every time a town run – to Trenton or Gallatin or Chillicothe – is needed.

I quickly learned that when a new, young Amish friend calls and says cheerily, "Hi David. Are you doing anything later this afternoon?" chances are not good that they're looking for someone to help them finish up the homemade ice cream. Nope, they need something in town.

And sometimes that works out great for all. Car rides are the best platforms for conversation. But my standard, mock serious answer when I drop them home and they ask what they owe me is, "Oh, a hundred bucks will do it."

I don't want to get on the driver call list.

Abe is an exception. Abe is my 2$^{nd}$ brain. The time we spend together is fun but we always have business to discuss – production logistics, inventory planning, new product ideas, old product improvements. We can easily fill an hour and still have several topics to go.

Abe's call that Susie could use the midwife now came in the early evening. I picked up Barb Beechy, mother of dear Rosemary who spent a lot of time with Grandma in her last years, wife of Joni, the sawmill owner too nice to say 'no' to our crazy requests.

Barb came out with an overnight bag that surely contained more than clothing and toiletries. What does a midwife do? I hadn't a clue.

But having witnessed and assisted hundreds of animal births I had a pretty good idea. I also had a pretty good idea of what can go wrong and how difficult it can sometimes be. My job was to be on call in case it became too difficult for Barb.

I had a book to read in the car. Time shifted into slow motion. Abe came out once or twice to give me a status report. I moved to the shop, sat in the comfy office chair and put my feet up on the desk.

Many slow hours later Abe came out and yelled to me that they had a healthy baby.

"Boy?" I asked.

"Girl."

"Congratulations!"

It took me a long time to stop calling their kids the "girlies" after their fourth child, a boy, was born eighteen months later. Although I declined the offer to be the driver on call for this next child, I started having a fun thought which I kept to myself: I had the fantasy that if they had a boy they would name him David. And if they named him David they would give him the middle name Andrew after Abe's next younger brother, who had died six years earlier. He would be a David Andrew. Just like me. But they didn't know my middle name.

So I had the rare opportunity to get one up on Abe the next time he called to tell me Susie had a baby.

"It's a boy. Guess what we named it!" I could hear the excitement in his voice.

"David Andrew?"

Silence.

"Did I already call you?" His poor mind had failed him.

I could have tormented him more with, "Don't you remember?" but instead, "No, I just knew," came out, along with, "You didn't know Andrew was my middle name too, did you?"

"Serious?"

"Yup."

"Well, I'll be."

And after that when the girlies were yakking away in their Deutsch language that I couldn't understand, the very familiar, though highly accented, "David Andrew" resounded in every other sentence. Oh, they were excited to have a baby brother!

Even though he wasn't "my baby" like Rachel Ann, I couldn't help but have a special soft spot for this newcomer named after me, even if the naming was accidental!

Now try to imagine my frustration as I watched this family develop from before marriage to four beautiful blonde-headed, rosy-cheeked wee ones that I was not able to talk to. It was only my problem because they talked to me as if I could understand them.

"David Schafer! Yak-yak-yak-yak." Beth brought me a crayon drawing and told me what it was.

"Oh, my Beth. That's beautiful!"

Then another sincere string of yak-yaks with an inquisitive ending would require me to look up to Mom or Dad for the explanation. Then, after my answer in English, Beth beams and goes back to her creativity.

Beth and Susannah seemed to have no problem understanding me. I was the only dull one and they forgave that.

Then one magical day a beaming Beth rattled off a complete sentence to me in English! I was astonished and thrilled that we were suddenly on speaking terms that worked for me. As a "scholar," Beth, like all of her Amish classmates, receives all instruction in English. Soon, Susannah, too, was speaking English learned from her big sister.

The language barrier protects their innocence for their first four or five years of life and insures they are deeply rooted in the Amish culture. Turning into a scholar opens up the "English" world to the young Amish and how they must devour the new world of picture books with words that suddenly have meaning.

It's Thanksgiving weekend as I write. Abe and his family – now a total of seven with Paul Abraham added to the crew - took a rare bus trip to Virginia to spend a little time away seeing distant relatives. The chicken plucker factory, going on six years old, shut down for the first time in history.

Abe didn't ask me about it;, he told me. "We'll ship again on Monday after I'm back. It's a slow time of year." He had it all worked out.

I nodded my head.

He grinned, "And if anybody needs anything urgently, here's a key." He handed me one of the sacred keys.

"Oh," he said, smiling more and pretending to just remember, "and you can make a copy and keep it!"

# Chapter 19
## James

A FEW SUMMERS AGO, when the evenings were still and the humidity and wind just right, we could hear the distant clip-clip-clop... clip-clip-clop... of a horse galloping along the meadow road and we knew that James was training. Straight from eight honest hours at Solly's sawmill, he'd get right to horse training, his side job, before anything else. That kind of discipline and determination was pure James right up to the moment of his untimely death.

Norman Ropp had told us that we'd like Jake and all his family when we bought the place. Jake Graber, older brother to Syl, who built the first Featherman chicken pluckers with me, had moved to Jamesport from Ohio with his large family. Not only were they large in number with five girls and four boys, but they were large - as in very tall — as well.

Jake and Mary are slightly above average height, but the four boys all topped out well over six foot. Danny Joe, the eldest, biggest, and funniest of a family with a keen sense of humor, has a bumpkin presentation that belies the depth of self-taught book wisdom within. Whether his dyslexia is a ruse or just the worst case I've ever seen, I still haven't figured out. In either case he seems to enjoy it.

Stephen, the next boy, has an eagle eye, is more reserved, and is as tall as Danny Joe but slighter. The hunting instinct – strong in all Amish boys – reaches the avid level in quiet Stephen.

Then come James and John, peas in a pod. Handsome, chiseled faces and almost as tall as their big brothers. Well, young Johnny's still growing as I write and may be a seven footer by the time you read this.

As with all my Amish friends, it took a while to get to know Jake's family. Even though they were a short distance away, we rarely drove on their road and saw each other only occasionally. I don't remember how, but someone hit upon the idea of a chess night at their place.

It turned out to be chess, scrabble, and rook night with Verna and Menno Graber, neighbors who live between Jake's place and ours; their youngest son, Ora (pronounced Or-ee), also well over six feet tall; and sometimes their girls, Mary Lynn and Barbara. Add Menno's bunch to Jake and Mary and their four boys and Jake and Mary's daughters still living at home - Marie, Sarah, Anna, and Laura – and any drop-in guests, and that came to quite a big crowd. Add up the inches with six six-footers in the bunch and it was a really big crowd.

The Amish are used to a lot of humanity within one household. Jake and Mary didn't even have to get out extra tables. The house was permanently arranged to seat 16 at one sitting with two tables pulled together.

I started really looking forward to our chess and scrabble nights on Tuesdays. Jake and Verna and I were stalwarts at the scrabble board. Mary or one of the boys or girls often took the fourth rack. Jake's family is very verbal. They are even more voracious readers than the average Amish family. Without television and radio and computers it's either books or games or early to bed in an Amish home. Their eldest daughter, Esther, won the Holmes County, Ohio, spelling bee in her pre-Jamesport days.

Anywhere from one to three chessboards will have combatants and spectators hunched over them on either side of the scrabblers. And every so often a game of rook (cards without face cards) is also played.

I especially like the rook games because they are so spirited. The worn and bent cards are slapped down on the table in rapid sequence of play after the careful bidding process is complete. Then lots of laughter and 'oohs' and 'ahhs' of disappointment or delight punctuate the end of each round and lead to discussions of different lead "what ifs" and tactical variations that were – or might have been – employed. Sometimes they will slip into their Deutsch (pronounced dietch as in righteous) which is always a treat to me since common courtesy dictates English be spoken within earshot of a non-Amish person. I take it as acceptance of my presence and try to pick up another word or two.

The scrabble is friendly. We use dictionaries and word lists and no time constraints. Jake holds the record for highest word score with "shafting" hitting the triple-triple and fetching him over 200 points on one word. At the time it seemed like a fitting word for those of us who lost big.

As much fun as the scrabble and rook games are, we still call it chess night and that's the main event. Besides the four Jake Graber boys and Menno Graber's Ora and me – the regulars – other chess players pop in from time to time. Big Johnny Rainey, a feed salesman and driver for the Amish, was a contender for a while. Bishop David Bontrager, as lively a fellow as you'll ever meet, is always a welcome guest. Several of the nearby young boys also come over from time to time.

With three or four boards set out on the table and at least twice as many players there is a quiet concentration interrupted only by the sound of pieces being moved and captured and the scrabbler's noise - almost a library atmosphere. Of course that is after all the local news is discussed thoroughly with all the men weighing in heavily and the women deferring or making light, gentle comments. Count on towering Menno to make a one-sentence comment as dry as toast that will bring a thunder of laughter from all, especially Danny Joe.

Danny Joe and Menno are like matches and gasoline together. I've seen them go back and forth for twenty minutes with Menno not so much as looking up from his cards or barely cracking a smile while Danny Joe is nearly crying from laughing so much and feeding Menno the counter lines. My personal Abbot-and-Costello routine – two names that mean nothing to them.

When Menno is not there, Danny Joe, if he's not completely absorbed in a book, will provide the entertainment solo.

"Hey Da-ave," he says slowly, eyes already twinkling with delight at the punch line to come.

"Did you hear about the three blonde girls studying to be crimninologists?" It was already hysterical with his gleeful butchering of the five-syllable word.

And he'd tell a variation of a joke I had heard in Junior High School and even though I knew the punch line and the joke was ancient, just hearing Danny's plodding delivery complete with dyslectic gyromotations made it twice as funny as before. And he could keep telling them forever.

Jake is a world-class storyteller, but Danny Joe could be a rock-star comic if he wanted. Danny Joe has stretched the three- to five-year average length of Rumspringa to double figures. He could leave the Amish to do something like that. But I doubt he will.

For James, Rumspringa offered the insane sport of bull riding. James, the quiet, the studious, the gentle. It just made no sense. But James marched to his own drummer. Over the chessboard James was not like his brothers. All the Graber brothers are blessed with deep-thinking minds, but in addition to that, James played the options over and over in his head before making a move. It resulted in his dominance at chess. (Ora did give James a tough run after Ora broke his leg and played battery-operated chess almost non-stop for three weeks.)

Youngest brother Johnny once told me in his sincere way that James was always trying to match his big brothers. Anything he took up he'd focus on until he reached their level. And then he'd go beyond.

I guess bull riding was logical after he ran out of challenges. We outsiders can't comprehend the changing dynamics of a young life, sheltered and kept close at home in the country and then, upon his or her seventeenth birthday, given freedoms he or she had never had. No curfew. Cell phone if they want. Car, if they are gutsy enough. The parents attempt to turn their back on behavior lacking good judgment, knowing that their youth must come to their own decisions. It's an extremely wise system. The fact that over 80% of all Amish youth choose to stay Amish validates it.

James had a car but I never knew it until after the accident. I've seen other Rumspringa cars around – cheap, small rigs that just barely passed their last inspection, parked during the week along a remote pasture. James had been getting rides to his rodeo competitions at first but for some reason he decided to get his own vehicle.

It looked like James was finished with rodeo after a bull came down on him and put him in intensive care. I didn't see him for three weeks after the accident but when I did he looked like a ghost – skinny and pale and slow moving. His liver damage produced a yellow cast on his skin. Still he managed his charming, humble, smile and positive attitude. Surely his family, like me, were satisfied that the severity of his accident would spell the end to this crazy phase. But soon, to the horror of all of us who loved him, he was training again.

Well, that was James. "Quit" was not in his vocabulary. James began coming to yoga classes with us. This may not sound strange to the outsider but yoga to a twenty-year old Amish boy has no appeal. Unless he is in training. James realized he needed more flexibility and an additional strengthening routine. Of course the balance gained in yoga wouldn't hurt a bit either.

After he ripped out a pair of britches, Sue, the instructor, found an old pair of long-legged sweatpants in a thrift shop and left them at the studio for James. Quiet, gentle, sincere. That's how I remember James in yoga, across the chessboard, and in conversation. There just wasn't anything to not like about him. I can't help but think of King James and Saint James.

Verna Graber called us early one morning with the shocking news of James's death a few hours earlier on the highway coming home from a rodeo in Iowa. It was snowing and the roads were bad; he passed a semi, slid off to the right shoulder, and came back on the road into the path of the semi. It wasn't a bull that got him but the similarity is unavoidable.

What remains of a being when the flesh, blood, and bones of him are gone speaks volumes. When Grandma Gladys passed, twenty years of living with her critical eye and reprimanding tongue, her decreasing mobility and uncooperative body, were swept away when I sensed her essential nature. The surprising image of a dancer in white, effortlessly and gracefully leaping and gliding came to me. The image of freedom and joy may have been my own creation, or was I tapping into something else?

When my lifetime mate, Buckley the wonder dog, left us, so strong was his essence that it was as if his devoted, un-judging presence was stronger than ever. Alice and I were deeply moved by it.

With James, the defining and lingering image is easy. It stems from an encounter in the magic meadow on one of his training rides. We met on the road, he on horseback and I afoot, and chatted a while. I offered that Alice and I were going to be taking a trip soon and would he or his brothers be willing to do some chores while we were gone?

His instant, certain, willing, and unselfish response defines the eternal, beautiful essence of James for me.

"Why David, we'd do anything for you."

James, more than any other person I've known, consistently showed the world the best of himself.

# CHAPTER 20
# MY AMISH PARTNER IN CRIME

L EST I AM accused of only portraying the idyllic side of my Amish friends and adopted community, I will, at great risk to my already shaky position at the edge of that community, relate a dark story of serious criminal activity. This is a true story about a famous crime that took place in the heart of Poosey during the bitter cold January of 2008.

It involves a family's narrow escape from a burning house, rushed international jet travel, a relative on her death bed, weeks of legal manipulation, mysterious land deeds, secret disposal of hazardous wastes, and dogged intense criminal investigation.

To protect his identity and the slim chance of his innocence I won't tell you exactly which Joe Burkholder this story is about. Let's just refer to him as Joe Edward. The one at Sherwood Crossing. With the furniture store.

The year 2007 ended with blustery northern winds and temperatures falling well below zero in north Missouri. Somewhere between the first minutes of 2008 and the hazy dawn of that bone-chilling morning, Joe Edward's house caught fire. Whether the wind forced sparks through the flue or the flue became hot enough to set fire to the wall, no one knows. By the time Joe Edward's fire alarms woke him, he had just enough time to raise his wife and two little girls from bed and escape with the nightclothes on their backs. The house quickly burned to the ground; they lost everything.

No, he didn't set the fire. Joe's criminal mind works in other ways besides arson.

By 8:00 am the community machine was fully engaged. Our first call came around 7:00 am from our neighbor Verna Graber, Joe's partner in the Quilt Shop. We received four more calls before noon. All small town folk look out for their neighbors, but what happens in an Amish community must be seen to be believed. NASA could take lessons on project coordination.

In three weeks (of very challenging weather) Joe's family moved back in to their new, larger home. On the same spot. Yes, that's right, three weeks. The burned debris was cleared away. A new cement foundation was poured. A three-story home was framed in. Brick chimney layed. House roofed, windowed, sided, insulated, floored, drywalled, painted, plumbed, fixtures installed, propane lines put in. They hung new hand-made curtains and moved in furniture. In three weeks. In freezing cold weather. There are witnesses. True story.

I don't care how wealthy a non-Amish person you may be, there is no way you could move into a new house on the site of your old one within months let alone 21 days! It can only happen through community coordination in a community full of home-building crews. Every crew in the Jamesport community scheduled their time slot tightly to complete their designated tasks. Often several crews were on the job at once. Always there were volunteer workers who weren't on carpenter or cement or roofing crews to pitch in. All work is donated, and though many men work on the job, nearly that many women are keeping them all fed and watered.

Several foremen are designated to coordinate supplies. Drivers who make their living shuttling Amish around ("hauling Amish" is the unflattering but commonly used term) are on call and running all day. Delivery trucks are in and out. I was called by Menno to pick up some cement-working supplies from Menno's shed. Joe's phone shack was command central and rarely unoccupied.

The money to pay for the new house supplies was there immediately. Many people made small cash donations but it is the Amish insurance system working quickly and efficiently that allowed such a rapid rebuilding to happen.

Amish insurance is unique and brilliant and all handled within the community. Using the county property assessments as a base, all property owners must contribute to an insurance fund. They have some latitude for insuring on the high end or low end. In other words, they can assess their property up or down and vary their payment to be insured a little more or less. But they must insure within an agreed-upon range.

An insurance committee sees that a reasonable amount of money remains in the insurance fund. When there is a big loss in the community such as for Joe's house fire, the kitty has to be built up again. It really is as if each member contributes to rebuild the house and that's how they think of it. It is totally transparent insurance. You know everyone in your insurance pool and what they have filed claims for. And the claim filers know all those who helped pay for their loss. And you know your insurance man and the company behind him are not getting rich off your premiums because he's not paid at all. It's a system that encourages individual responsibility and safety but provides a no-fail safety net and quickly lends a hand. Everyone knows it might be his or her loss next time.

I first learned of Amish insurance when friend Ernie Kauffman had a brooder fire and lost several hundred chickens along with his big brooder house. Another Amish man said to me casually, "My share was $40." He explained it to me and I was so impressed I offered Ernie $40 then and there. If only it was that easy to join the Amish insurance system.

I saw it in action again the morning after high winds ruined our first prairie schooner, a plastic pipe and tarp shelter that had one-day old baby chicks in it. We had just sold and transferred it over to Freeman and Sara, Ernie's' daughter and son-in-law. That was no small task for a structure measuring 15 feet wide by 40 feet long by seven feet high.

We knew Sara had gone into labor the evening of the storm and they were in the hospital. Freeman had received the baby chicks but I wondered if the schooner was secured to the ground. I had forgotten to do it and Freeman had his mind on other things. Winds this high could damage a schooner whether anchored or not. Alice and I drove to their farm at 12:30 am and found a disaster scene. The schooner had rolled and the frame looked like the bleached bones of Moby Dick, the tarp torn and twisted around them.

By the truck headlights we scooped up hundreds of soaked baby chicks and dried them in our pickup with the heater running full blast.

Returning early the next morning to survey the damage by light, there were three older gentlemen already there huddled in discussion and if not for their clipboard I would have guessed they were spectators. The insurance committee was already on the job. And Freeman was covered.

The strength of a system shows itself best under pressure. An Amish community may appear quaint, old-fashioned, slow-paced, and cumbersome to those of us who only view it out our car windows. We see horse-drawn vehicles, clothes on the lines, and no utility poles. But put that community under pressure and you will see stunning results that simply cannot be reproduced elsewhere.

As Alice and I drove by the Burkholder house every time we went to town, we were treated to a fast-forward display of home construction. We would dutifully give progress reports to each other and friends.

"Well, David, Menno and Elvan finished up the cement work this morning."

"Chet's and John's crews got it completely framed today."

"The roof's on and Carl's putting the windows in."

"Johnny has the chimney almost finished."

"Ferman's crew is putting on siding."

Across the area, folks lost their building crews for a day or two as they pulled out to help rebuild the lost home in Jamesport. Sure it cost everybody money. The foreman had to pack up from one site and re-schedule material deliveries to two sites. His crew understood they were going to work for a day or two without pay. (It might be their home next time.) It's understood with Amish that these things happen and it not only activates the insurance system, it throws the whole community into high gear. They rally. They are at their best and most efficient. Our ex-Amish neighbor Mandy stated it matter of factly, "They're really good at this."

The helpers who threw the sheetrock and insulation trim in the ditch along the magic meadow where Alice and I first fell in love with our farm were doing the best they could at the time; they just made one mistake. They got caught. It seemed simple enough to add more to the ditch; folks have been putting stuff in it for years. No problem.

I was shocked and a little angry the first time I saw the pink insulation hanging like shirts on a clothesline from the limbs of the trimmed brush that always topped the pile. As I drove by I also saw the sheetrock pieces. I thought, "They could at least have made an effort to hide it a little."

Then I realized where it probably came from and lost my bitterness. I knew whoever did it was operating in high gear, hurrying to get back to the job. And I knew that it would all be covered soon when either Gary or we did more trimming of the road or around our properties and covered it up with brush. I almost stopped to tidy it up but decided to do it later.

This ditch filling program had been going on for nearly a decade. Well, ever since Gary and Carol and Alice and I had moved in at the turn of the century. Richard said we should have bladed back into our pasture – the magic meadow – to bring the road away from the creek and, of course, he is right. It was a very dangerous road hazard. With sixty-foot bluffs carved onto the south side, the creek was working its way back across the meadow and chewing into the road. An abrupt twelve-foot drop from road to creek bed put us all to the task of mending the cut.

Richard, doing duty more as a good neighbor than the township road maintainer, contributed. Gary made the biggest effort. Before he traded the property to the Missouri Department of Conservation (MDC), he hired a track-hoe to build a long dam eight feet high to keep the creek from running against the road. It must have cost him a lot.

We all began filling up the hole with materials both natural and not. Someone dropped in a truckload of broken up cement. There were old rolls of barbed wire. Even a road tube, as they call culverts here. The unspoken rule was to cover whatever went in with brush or rock. We all loved the winding one-lane road, loved the conserved land on the south bluff and had all chipped in to clear brush on the MDC side of the road to open it up for gravel trucks.

The MDC wasn't excited about opening up the new road. For a while we thought they would pony up a good chunk of the expense for the first gravel like the rest of the neighbors did. Even though it is a county road, 55th Ave – the unimaginative, grid-based name given for easy location in an emergency – had to have its first load of gravel paid for by the adjacent land owners. That's just the way it works. After that, the maintenance cost comes out of the county treasury.

We called the MDC, told them we were opening the dirt road at the north edge of the 6000-acre Poosey Conservation Area, and asked if they would help contribute to the base layer of gravel. It was a long shot. There were no designated entry sites to the conservation area – their criteria for funding gravel. And although the MDC is the beneficiary of a 1/10 sales tax specifically ear-marked for parks and recreation – a great boon to the state's recreational areas - their gravel budget didn't have any funds in it for our new road.

We love having the conservation land as a border. We chose our home property based upon it. We are protective of the public land. I contacted them once when a large pond dam was about to fail and they promptly sent equipment to repair it. We are sentinels preventing illegal hunting activities. We are caretakers picking up beer cans and other trash. Mostly, we are the ultimate appreciators.

The new MDC man saw us differently.

"Are you David Schafer?"

"Yes, I am," I answered seriously and formally to match him.

He introduced himself then said, "I suppose you know why I'm here."

I didn't see a plate of brownies anywhere so I quickly dismissed a get-to-know-your-new-agent visit.

The timing could not have been worse. I was just finishing up doing the evening horse chores for Alice and was looking forward to the one bright spot of this unusually depressing day. The day before, we had received a call that resulted in Alice booking an emergency flight to Mexico to see her Mom alive for the last time. I had driven her to the airport at 3:30 that morning.

It was a cold, cloudy, windy January day and I wasn't dressed warmly enough to do the horse chores let alone visit with whoever was driving up our long driveway. I waited and when I saw the logo on the side of the truck I knew it was Terry's replacement. He looked young.

"No," I said truthfully, I didn't know why he was there. But if I'd taken a guess I would have guessed right; darn the pink insulation.

Terry Truttman, the previous MDC man overseeing Poosey Conservation Area, had been a friend for years. His wife Lisa had given Alice many riding lessons in the magic meadow, not 50 yards from "the scene of the crime." Terry had driven that road dozens of times, surely seen the brush, the rocks, the culvert, the scraps from our home construction – all put in and covered over prior to MDC ownership – and never said a peep about it.

The new MDC man was lookin' to round up all the outlaws of north Missouri and put 'em behind bars. I reckon me and Joe's time done run out.

"I found your name on a piece of paper in a pile of garbage along the creek. Do you have any idea how it got there?"

Time froze. I seriously considered saying, "I cannot tell a lie Officer Obie. I put that piece of paper under that pile of garbage." I could have grabbed my guitar and played him practically the entire song, complete with accurate finger picking, four-part harmony, and glossy pictures with circles and arrows and explanations on the back of each one.

But I had to put humor and Arlo Guthrie's "Alice's Restaurant" aside. This was no time for levity. I knew there was no paper. We never put any paper down there. But how did he get my name? The mailbox said Schafer/ Dobbs. Did he just know we lived here? Could he have made a phone call to play this bluff game?

"Can I see that paper?" I asked politely.

No, that wasn't necessary. "Did I put any waste materials in that ditch or not?"

"I have put a lot of material in there over the years," I said, choosing my words carefully.

"All the neighbors have been trying to prevent that wash out from cutting into the road ever since we opened the road ten years ago - before it was Conservation Department property."

My appeals to the history, the neighborhood involvement, my good citizenship fell on deaf ears.

"What materials?" He was closing in for the kill.

Well here we go, I thought, but I wasn't about to lie. Surely he'd see that we've spent a lot of time protecting that spot, that we're upstanding citizens.

"Well, over the years we've put a lot of brush in there. Just recently we added an addition to our house," I pointed toward the warmth of my home, "and we had to take out a wall. We put some of the broken stone and straw bales and some old two-byes and" (this was going to cancel out any straw bale "natural" brownie points I might have made) "a little bit of tin in it." He didn't seem to care about any of those materials.

"What about insulation or sheetrock?"

I could've wrung somebody's neck and mentally kicked myself for not stopping to take in the pink laundry. Alice and I were protective of the ditch since it was right across from the magic meadow. Plus we almost owned that side of the road once. It's complicated.

When we first bought the property in 1997, Norman was certain he owned a few acres across the county line. We read and re-read and re-re-read the property boundary lines and they didn't make sense; the property lines didn't close. The surveyors Norman hired couldn't figure them out. Finally, in a stroke of genius, Alice surmised that a clerk had been copying the

164

description and at a certain point skipped to another line that also ended in "county line road," leaving out a line or two; it could have accounted for the error. Putting a line or two in would close the property lines neatly. But alas...

We didn't buy the acreage across the creek. Our neighbor, Gary Ellis, did. All of us neighbors cleared the trees back from the mud road so that gravel trucks could come in. There were Gary, Norman, Alice and me, and Richard Morris, who also (in perfect universal orchestration) had the job of Madison township road maintainer. That's the guy who clears the road of snow, sees that gravel is laid when needed, blades out the ditches, puts in new culverts, and generally does all those essential and thankless tasks required of gravel roads in the country. Richard is tops at it.

It took quite a few days of cutting and hauling the brush with chain saws and trucks to turn a mud track into a cleared swath big enough to be a legal county road. The best spot for the brush was this steep cut along the roadside in the bend in our magic meadow, referred to as "the ditch." We spoke to Richard about this spot at length.

"It's bad," Richard shook his head and squinted his blue eyes. "It could take the road." Richard was hard of hearing and had mumbled from the time he was a boy. We had to listen hard and lean close, which was fun because he was so delightful.

Richard had taken to Alice from the get-go and vice versa. She would yuck it up with him and slap the chest pockets of his bib overalls. Richard would spin some teasing yarn then pull back and squint for the ensuing reaction. Whenever we encountered Richard driving the faded-yellow grader, dressing the gravel on the roads, we had to pull over and chew the fat. Richard would have wondered why we were upset with him if we didn't. With Richard we could count on a 20-minute discussion of recent township decisions, positions on the board, quarry problems, and general neighborhood gossip.

One time Alice thought she owed Richard some money. It was a small amount. She pulled out a bill and stuffed it in his chest pocket but he was fast as a rabbit and caught her hand before she got it in. A good-natured wrestling match ensued for five minutes, raising dust on the road from all their scuffing and leaving them bent over double, huffing and laughing. Then, after a few breaths, Alice tried to stuff the bill in Richard's seat pocket and the whole crazy contest played out again. Alice is tougher than a boiled owl and can out-grapple many bigger than her, but Richard, even in his 70s, was an even match.

Our new Conservation man had no idea about the opening of this road. No idea about our cutting brush on their side. No idea that Gary had once owned that land and paid for some expensive earthwork to further protect the wash area. No idea that Gary traded the Conservation Department that little property for a small one adjacent to his home, giving both contiguous properties. For all the Conservation man knew the road was 100 years old, we moved in last week and dumped all the stuff in there yesterday.

Righteous indignation was lifting me up to a dangerous pulpit. Why… he didn't know I was a champion of healing the land…that I had hosted distinguished members of the Conservation Department many times on our previous farm. He had no idea we were among the first in the area to plant warm season grasses…or that we left 15-foot wide "wildlife corridors" in between our pastures. I was really winding up now. He didn't know that our idea of vacationing was weeklong tracking classes and wildlife watching.

Would the knowledge that we had endured four-day vision quests in these very woods, staying that whole time – except for nature calls - within a 10-foot circle, connecting intimately with this land have made a difference?

Nope.

A saint and a pickpocket pass on the street. The saint sees a child of God on his unique and perfect path. The pickpocket sees more pockets.

The agent didn't see my sub-divided pastures or wildlife corridors or healthy grasslands or tree-lined driveway. He didn't notice my solar panels or pipes delivering roof water to an elevated pond. He didn't care about my straw bale home (except that it didn't have pink insulation). I could have been the green guy of the century, the Nobel Prize winner for green living, but he didn't see it. He saw a litterbug.

"No. We didn't put any insulation or sheet rock in there."

"Are you sure?"

By now I was getting cold and tired. I probably took a little longer to answer those three words than would ordinarily be socially acceptable as I summed up the young man in the truck who was making my life miserable.

I explained to him that the type of insulation we used was a grey cellulose that is blown in, not laid down in rolls.

He was like a dog on a bone. He asked about the sheetrock. I told him the name of the person we hired for that job and that he hauled it off when he was finished.

Conservation man decided I might be telling the truth and asked if I knew who put that insulation and sheetrock in there. This was another cause for a pause. Did I know who put it there? Hmmm....

Another way of looking at the question was, "Did I have any idea who carelessly left the mess near my property that was responsible for my having a most unpleasant conversation in the freezing cold when I could have been exercising, relaxing, and centering myself in a yoga class?"

If ever there was a nasty temptation to rat on someone this was it. But I truly didn't know.

"Somebody else building a house, I suppose."

"Are there other people around here building?" He must have driven right by Joe's on the way in. It was as busy as rush hour in downtown Kansas City. Could he have missed it?

What the heck. Maybe the house fire would soften him. "Well, there's Joe Burkholder whose house burned down two weeks ago."

I didn't know for sure if the mess was from Joe's but I would have bet on it and the agent would have tortured the same information out of any of the other non-litterbug neighbors. Plus, on the blood trail now, he couldn't miss it on his way out.

Apparently that was all the information he needed from me. It was down to business now. "I'm going to have to give you a ticket."

You could have knocked me over with a feather.

"You WHAT? You've got to be kidding!"

He wasn't and he did. I was fuming mad. Mad at the injustice, the lack of circumspection, and the silly "name on the paper under the garbage" ruse. My rage lasted about 10 seconds and, fortunately, I didn't say anything during that time.

After ten seconds I took a long view. I practiced being saintly towards this pickpocket who was right on his path. He was the new law enforcement guy in town. Just out of school. He was out to let everyone know he was a serious conservation agent with the emphasis on agent.

He had a big responsibility overseeing not only this 6000-acre conservation area but a much larger range as well. He wanted to do the right thing and let people know from the get-go that the new agent wouldn't tolerate law-breakers. I couldn't blame him a bit. I too might have been a "by the book guy" in his situation.

It reminded me of long time family friend LeRoy (not LEE roy but l'ROY) Miller telling me that when he was first out of law school he came back to Grundy County to work for the prosecuting attorney's office. This was back in prohibition days when Poosey was full of moonshiners. LeRoy said he went hunting for stills out near where we lived several times but never could find any. Then, smiling broadly, he quickly added, "If I found one today I'd have a drink with 'em."

Maybe someday I'll have a drink with the Conservation agent. What we have in common is much greater than what we don't.

I also realized that I had brought this episode on myself. At the time we did it I didn't feel right putting tin and boards full of nails in there. They didn't amount to much. They would soon be covered over. And they would help stabilize the bank. Those were the rationalizations, but we shouldn't have put them there and I knew it.

In all likelihood the previous agent – our friend Terry - would have taken action over the current mess too. I actually got to where I felt a little sorry for these conservation agents having to do this type of dirty work.

Filling out the ticket form took him two eternities. It was obviously his first time to catch a real, live, confessed litterbug. I invited him into the warmth of the house. I was visibly shaking from cold and adrenalin by then. He declined, probably picturing his demise from blunt object trauma as I graciously ushered him in before me. And then – the ultimate revenge – I'd hide his body in the ditch!

At long last he handed me the ticket. I read it. There was a court date. What was I supposed to do? Was it like a traffic violation? Do I send money? How much? He wasn't sure what happened next either.

I'll admit I was not at my keenest but at the end of our getting-to-know-you chat I had the distinct impression that I was to notify him when I had removed all the materials for which I was responsible and then my slate would be wiped clean.

Well, I was in for another surprise.

On my late drive to yoga class, I passed the usual buzz of activity at Joe's house. Besides the swarm of black buggies and horses and pick-up trucks that were always there since the fire, I noticed the agent's pick-up. Sorry Joe, but it looks like we're partners in crime.

- - -

About a week later, after Alice had returned from Mexico, we heard a racket down in the valley and went to investigate. A pick-up and trailer were parked at the ditch and dumping! No wait. They were hauling material up out of the ditch. We parked next to Annette, Joe's driver.

"Well, looks like you had a talk with the agent too," I said to Joe, who was handing sheetrock up to several other Amish guys to throw into the truck. The trailer was already full.

"Oh, did he get you, too?" Joe said with his award-winning smile.

"Yep," I said climbing down the hillside to haul some of my evidence away. "Gave me a ticket, too. You?"

"Yes."

"What are we supposed to do? Did he tell you?"

"I don't know for sure. Clear out the sheetrock and insulation. Then we might have to go to court."

"Did he tell you that?"

"No. But somebody I talked to did."

"I think I better call a lawyer. Do you want to go in on it if I do?"

"Yes."

I wasn't sure if Amish were even allowed to use attorneys. I know they avoid litigation like the plague.

We filled our trucks and trailers and talked about the crime. Turns out the agent and Joe had an even more interesting conversation than I did. Joe told him that yes, the sheetrock and insulation were from his construction but he had no idea who put it there. Agent man had a pretty hard time believing that statement, but Joe held fast claiming a lot of people were doing a lot of things and he really didn't know who took the waste to the ditch. With forty or fifty men doing various tasks at any given time, and Joe making hundreds of decisions, hiring and traveling with drivers to pick up materials several times each day, it is perfectly believable. So Joe took the bullet and got the ticket for himself.

As young Amish men go, Joe is at the top of his class. Good-looking and confident, ambitious, community-minded, Joe is liked by everyone. He created a booming furniture business out of his own hustle and determination.

It quickly expanded beyond his space and he bought another property and built a huge building to contain a show floor and workshop shared with Menno and Verna Graber's Sherwood Quilt Shop under the same roof.

Not only is Joe a smart businessman at a young age, but he's also one of the biggest volunteers to help organize Jamesport events – festivals, quilt and antique auctions, improvement of community buildings, etc. He's a git-'er-done type guy. If you have to choose a partner in crime, I recommend Joe.

We shared phone messages through the next couple of weeks updating each other on what we knew. I couldn't reach the agent. The Conservation Department knew nothing. The agent worked out of his home and was never there or at the office. He didn't return my messages. The prosecuting attorney's office knew nothing. I finally left a message saying we had picked up all the trash and I had a receipt from the landfill to show where I'd taken it. I would mail a copy and I assumed that was the end of the matter unless I heard otherwise.

'Otherwise' came in the form of a "missed court date" letter from Livingston County! I went into full battle mode. I phoned and apologized to the courthouse pleading ignorance; I did the same to the prosecutor's secretary – a waste of time; then I called the agent and let him have it. I felt more and more like a real criminal; I briefly entertained some truly criminal thoughts.

I called an attorney recommended by another attorney and told him as short a version of my personal "Alice's Restaurant" story as I could. He calmly said, "Don't worry; litter cases never get to trial."

"What?"

"Prosecutors hate litter cases; they all get thrown out. I'll take care of it." Turns out voters have an especially long and distasteful memory about litterbug cases. I don't know; the whole legal-schmegal maze is a mystery I have no interest in unraveling.

I gave my new legal representative Joe's name and address and asked that he include Joe in whatever it was he was going to do to "take care of it." Fill out some papers and give them to somebody else and send me a bill as far as I could tell.

Of course it drug on. "Should hear back any day now."

"Changed to next court date but we should get it dismissed before then."

All very positive sounding messages that left me feeling like a prisoner. Then I'd have to relate all the wishy-washiness to Joe who was getting all the non-info from me.

"Joe, will you go to court if we don't get it dismissed?"

"Yeah, I guess so." He laughed, "Do I have a choice?"

"No. Probably not."

Finally it concluded, months after the "crime." Our attorney called and said, "It got dismissed this morning. It's all over." And that was that.

Except that Joe and I each paid $200 in legal fees. I couldn't help imagining the attorneys "dismissing" our case over an evening beer after working out at the gym. It just seemed like such a hokey system all to the benefit of the attorneys. But American justice had been served so I should have been proud and patriotic.

A huge spring rain breached Gary's earthwork dam and brought the creek up against the cut, eroding it badly. The Conservation Department had placed a "No Littering" sign at the edge only weeks before. Now it was two feet lower and leaning sloppily.

That was wryly amusing to me for a while but then I decided that our boards and tin and Joe's sheetrock and insulation wouldn't have provided much extra protection to the cut.

Hey, next time you're in Jamesport why not run down to Sherwood Crossing and buy some furniture from Joe. And while you're there pick up a couple of gift copies of my book. It just might prevent two dangerous outlaws from returning to a life of crime!

# Chapter 21
# Tracker Influence

A T THE CITY Market one Saturday morning we were talking to a customer about visiting the farm. We invited her to stay in our teepee. Another customer heard the comment and said, "You have a teepee?"

"Yes, Scott, and you're welcome to come up and stay in it some time."

Scott paused in thought and said, "I'd like to come up, but I'd stay in a debris hut."

"What's a debris hut?"

And with that simple beginning a whole universe of intrigue opened up to Alice and me. In several years of apprenticeship with Scott not only did we learn to make and sleep in debris huts – basically squirrel nests on the ground – we learned to make fire with friction from plant materials and how to find water and various sources of food in the wild.

The four basics of survival – shelter, water, fire, and food – are not as important to Scott as are the spiritual skills used by the native people. With the spirit engaged we are connected to the world around us and aided in ways we can't conceive. Our senses stretch far beyond the norm.

Over the next several years we met with Scott and a few others many times. Scott's unique way of teaching slowly built our faith in our abilities to access a non-physical energy. Always we were in nature, away from the distractions of work, phone, and daily routine. We took our time, slowing down to nature's pace.

First we re-learned how to see. To replace tunnel vision we developed wide-angle vision so that a flicker of a deer tail 80 yards away was visible out of the corner of the eye. Just our expanded vision increased our awareness in an unexpected way.

Then we learned how to move through the landscape. Instead of crashing and tromping through the woods we learned to move slowly and gracefully, in harmony with the landscape. After a while it felt as if the bottoms of our feet had eyes of their own. There was no need to look down to place a foot. If a twig was underfoot we felt it through our soft footwear before cracking it, and then glided the foot to a "quiet" spot nearby.

We learned respect for the wildlife. When we walked in the woods we asked for permission from the wildlife just as you would knock on someone's door to ask permission into their house. That set a tone of humility, our deferential "woods" attitude.

With expanded awareness, slow, quiet movement, and a reverential respect, we could walk through the woods without disturbing the wildlife. Whenever we were together in nature, this is how we were. Whenever we failed to do all of these quieting, grounding, awareness-expanding exercises, the animals quickly let us know about it.

The animals are very demanding in that regard. Humans, on the other hand, are generally distracted and unaware. For example, five of us walked by a couple kissing on a remote park bench. We never changed our pace and they had no idea five people had walked by within touching distance.

Unimaginable things happened when we were together with Scott. He didn't teach us directly; he gave us exercises that allowed us to learn from the landscape. On one exercise I sat by a small tree I had chosen in a brushy area. Following Scott's instructions, I began to focus on my sight. I looked at the grasses and brush nearby, absorbing their colors and shapes and textures. When I felt I had absorbed them completely I looked further in to the distance and focused there. Finally, I studied the leaves of the farthest trees and then the clouds and sky.

Having catalogued everything visually I could, I then shifted to hearing. Trying to retain all the awareness of the objects I had studied visually, I overlaid the sounds. At first there were very few. A birdcall now and then. Then I heard more distant birdcalls. And then I was surprised to note the steady hum of the highway a few miles distant.

I became aware of the sounds my body makes. My breathing, my heartbeat, the soft rustle of clothing as I breathed. There were sounds everywhere! I catalogued them too as if in an amphitheater with each sound having its own precise location on the stage. This sensory sphere of sound awareness stretched out beyond most of my visual information. Birds and squirrels told stories all around me, as did the distant highway and farm equipment.

When I felt my sound library was complete I then concentrated on touch, trying to still be as aware of the sights and sounds as when I concentrated fully on each of them. Touch? What was there to touch? First I felt the ground through my legs. I felt the hard and soft spots. I sensed the temperature. I became aware of feedback up from my legs and all through my body.

I became aware of the touch of the air around my body, on my face, the feeling of it passing through my nose, throat, and lungs. The difference in temperature on the way in and out. I was amazed at how much "touch" information I had been subconsciously processing and was now consciously aware of.

Feeling out from my body, I sensed the tree I was leaning against. I felt the roughness of its bark against my back and then I felt the presence of a personality to it. I got the image of it behind me, though I hadn't taken a good look at it previously. I sensed its height and breadth. Imagining that I was part of the soil, I felt out through the ground into the plants around me.

I switched to the last of the senses Scott had told us to concentrate on: smell and taste, taken as one sense here. Again, it first seemed as if there was nothing to smell. Then I began to imagine certain qualities about the air. It was clean; it smelled clean. It was forest air. It smelled that way. Could I pick out the smells that made my mind think, "clean" and "forest?" I could conceive of the smell of earth and tree bark and decaying leaves. Was that just imagination? When I rolled the air in my mouth I felt I could sense the flavor of those smells.

All the while, I was attempting to keep my awareness of all the other senses expanded. I was a sensory tool totally open to all input, re-calibrated for heightened sensitivity.

Then a miracle happened. I heard a new sound. It was a soft rustle of the leaves on the ground at ten o'clock. The rustle grew louder. So did my heartbeat but I brought myself quickly back to the expanded awareness and connection with everything around me. In seconds a spotted fawn appeared through the brush, walking, sniffing the ground, slowly moving toward me. An identical fawn appeared behind it.

They ambled slowly through my field of sight, coming within a car's length of me. They moved out of my hearing range, their walk unchanged.

"Whoop, whoop!" Scott called us in to our meeting spot. Once we were gathered there, he asked, as always, "So what happened?"

He looked over at me and chuckled. "David?"

How did he always know? I related my story and asked why the fawns hadn't noticed me.

As usual Scott answered a question with a question. "Have you heard of invisibility?"

Things like that happened to all of us. Sometimes we were blocked and frustrated, but most of the time the information and experiences flowed.

In a very early exercise, Scott had us go to our sit spots and carve on sticks. We were to concentrate on the stick and put a lot of energy into them. After an hour he called us in and asked for our sticks. He then had us stand together in the middle of a small opening in the woods and blindfold ourselves.

"I'm walking in a circle around you about twenty yards away. I want you to enter the Sacred Silence and, when you're ready, walk to your stick and pick it up."

Simple. We took our deep breaths and exhaled to clear our minds and bodies and enter the state of relaxed concentration Scott called the Sacred Silence. One by one we started walking.

I hadn't a clue what to do or expect, but as with many of the exercises, I had to trust that I would somehow sense what to do. Soon I had a picture of a red airplane in my head. It was a bird's eye view and it looked to me like a direction indicator in an airplane's cockpit. It was pointing to one side, so I turned toward that direction and took a few tentative steps. Then, I felt myself get dizzy and off balance and I lost the picture.

"Well done, Clint….Good job Alice," I heard. The others had gone to their sticks on the first try.

Scott took my arm and guided me back to center. "Now go again," he said.

I breathed. I saw the plane. I walked. I staggered and lost it again.

"One last time," Scott said gently after planting me at the center again.

The pressure was on. Nobody liked to get skunked. I breathed deeply and centered myself. I saw the plane. I slowly straightened it out and steadily walked while it pointed straight ahead. Then I froze, disconnected.

After 20 seconds Scott gently said, "Pick up your stick, David."

I went down to my knees and reached wildly to my left. Peels of laughter came from the group as I ripped my bandana off and looked left to find my stick. They laughed harder. The stick was between my legs.

"Okay, journal about it." Scott always gave us time to process what happened for ourselves.

Becoming invisible and sensing objects we couldn't see were just two of many otherworldly skills we learned. It no longer seemed bizarre to us. But one simple exercise nearly scared me out of my skull.

Stealth and silence were critical skills. How, then, in a group, did you communicate with others? Scott showed us.

"We'll stalk down a trail together with me leading. When you see me stop, you'll know I planted a bubble there. Stop where I stopped and open up your mind to receive the information."

The stalk began with Scott taking a step every ten or twenty seconds. I was number two about five yards behind. After several minutes, Scott stopped for a minute. We all waited. He moved on and we each had a turn to move through his bubble.

I got completely into the spot, took a deep breath and nearly jumped out of my skin. I'm not a visual person. When I close my eyes nothing happens. I can imagine things but I don't "see" them. So when I get a vision I always know I'm not making it up. What I saw was a skull on fire!

I rushed out of the bubble and moved on. After we all had moved through the bubble we compared notes and came up with similar symbols. Scott's message had been, "Danger!"

After several years of doing these exercises with Scott we all had a much-altered picture of the world and our place in it. This world was more alive and exciting and it offered more possibilities and resources than we could have imagined. But there remained one big "exercise" that we all craved: the vision quest.

# CHAPTER 22
# SWEAT LODGE

WHY DID SO many primitive cultures in diverse locations choose to send their young adults to fast alone for four days with the expectation of receiving guidance from non-physical sources? This experience is the vision quest, a rite of passage accepted globally through most of history, but recently all but forgotten.

Scott helped us reconnect with that history. We spent long hours through day and night meditating and attempting to communicate with spirit. Like prayer, our meditations included gratitude. Unlike prayer, most of our time was spent listening for answers.

We opened a whole new universe to ourselves and wanted more of it. The most certain means of contact with the spirit was through fasting and eliminating all distraction. All the great religious leaders had done it. There must be something to it. Five of us were eager to quest and we found the ideal setting on our new farm.

The preparations were considerable. We wrote down our big questions and set our intentions half a year in advance, revisiting them regularly. Scott lectured us on the format and what to expect.

In early October Scott's friend Nick flew in to assist us. Scott and Nick were veterans at this and would assure a smooth time for us. On the first day we gathered wood and made an outdoor kitchen and a sweat lodge. That night we camped out on the land and inside our half-completed house.

The next day we found our individual quest sites. For me this involved wandering around the beautiful hills, still new to me, and sitting down once, twice, three times before I found the spot that felt right.

With two brief exceptions, we would be staying within a circular area ten feet in diameter. Exception one was our bathroom area. We cleared a short trail to that. Exception two was our "marker box." Every morning we were to take a stick, prepared beforehand, and place it in our marker boxes, also a short distance from our sites but out of our direct view. A little later in the day Scott or Nick would walk by to see that our sticks had been placed, which meant, "All is well."

We cleared brush on our trails and within our sites and each of us deposited four one-gallon containers of water under a tarp behind the trees we had chosen to sit against. Scott even told us to remove the labels from the containers.

"Your mind will be starved for stimulation. I don't want you reading the labels."

He even cautioned against "recreational peeing." That is, drinking a lot of water just to be able to get up a lot and walk to the bathroom area. That warning was to have serious consequences for several of us.

Besides water to drink, a tarp in case of rain, and our four marker box sticks, we had the layers of clothing we wore the morning we began the quest plus a sleeping bag we carried out.

It wasn't exactly a camping vacation and we were all a bit apprehensive. Starving the mind of stimulation is not necessarily a happy time. The Apaches called the vision quest, Nia ku, "little death," implying death of the ego.

We were hoping that at some point the ego mind would finally give in and spirit could enter. It sounded a little like going crazy on purpose but we all recently had experiences that, only a few years earlier, we would have said were crazy or impossible.

Our last pre-quest meal was at midday. We spent the rest of the day finishing the sweat lodge and building the immense fire to heat the stones for it. The sweat lodge would be the first for many of us and the first for all of us with Scott in charge. How could we not be apprehensive about going into a small, dark, very hot space with someone else in control? Some sweats we'd heard about sounded like machismo contests.

The atmosphere was solemn and as heavy as our work-weary arms. My body wanted food to replenish the energy just spent. Instead, we sat around a small fire near the sweat lodge for a long time waiting for Scott, and then we went over some final details with him.

As dark settled in Scott told us to get our swim suits on and bring a towel. The sweat lodge we made hardly seemed big enough for two people, let alone six! It measured four feet tall and ten feet in diameter. The fire pit in the center forced us to squeeze around the edges. A thin layer of fresh straw cushioned us a little.

Scott crawled in first, ducking low to go through the canvas flap that served as a door. He crawled to the left going all around the fire pit to wind up next to the door. We followed. I had the very lucky position of being last and, along with Scott, nearest the door.

Once we were all in Scott asked Nick to bring us stones. Nick had been vigilantly tending the fire all afternoon and evening. By now the stones glowed red. It was almost as if you could see through them. He picked them out of the coals with a pitchfork and, leaning into the lodge, placed them carefully in the fire pit one by one.

"Door!"

That was my cue from Scott to open or close the door. I closed the door.

Our small world shrank to consist of only seven glowing stones. Their surfaces flickered and flared like newly forming planets. Their stored heat – how can a rock hold so much heat? – pushed against my chest and head like a physical presence, causing sweat to break out instantly.

No words were spoken as the heat built. No one moved and the heat built more. My skin tickled with rivulets of sweat running down my face and shoulders, arms and legs. Scott materialized a cedar branch and swept it over the stones causing flares and pops and a sweet smell to fill our tiny space.

When he ladled out a cup of water and poured it over the rocks I realized how relatively comfortable I had been up to that point. The dry heat was manageable. The heat released with steam scalded the skin. It crept over me from the top down, singeing my ears and face first. It entered my nostrils and, if I breathed too deeply or too fast, it scorched my lungs.

Forcing myself to breath slowly was the beginning of a self-talk for survival: I know I can do this…it will end soon…we are all in this together…many people have done this before…

Scott had told us that at any time we could ask for the door and leave if we had to. Or lower our heads to breathe cooler air. He poured another cup of water that evaporated on the surface of the rocks with a hiss. I began a countdown in my mind.

Five…four…three…two…one…the scorching heat melted over my head and sent my mind screaming for the door but my body stayed still. It won't last long…we're all in this together…many have done this before…how can Scott be so cruel? …I know I can do this…

At some point Scott mercifully asked for the door and sweet, cool night air flowed in and over our drenched bodies for a few precious minutes.

"Is everyone okay?" Scott asked quietly.

Mumbles or no response indicated the affirmative. If someone had been slumped against his or her neighbor or babbling incoherently, I guess it would have been obvious.

"Door."

Again we went back into hell. This time we knew what we were in for. But that only made it worse. The next three sessions blurred together.

At some point during the four "doors" we sweated through that night, each of us, in our own way and time, surrendered. We gave up the need to control or fight or mentally scream. We were just there. We were simply experiencing the sensations. We were purging sweat and much more. Our minds turned off to various degrees, our bodies stopped fearing, and we became spectators of the sweat lodge and its effects on our bodies.

The sweat is a small death in itself, a mini-quest that can reveal mysteries and tune us in to things impossible for most of us to experience otherwise. A year earlier I sat in my first sweat lodge at the end of the Standard course with noted tracker and survivalist Tom Brown, Jr. There had been many people present and the heat not nearly so intense. But what I experienced there changed my view of the world.

First I saw images of a Native American, vivid images. I could have been making that part up. But then Tom sang a song in Apache that he had been taught by his aged mentor, Stalking Wolf, known to Tom as "Grandfather." I knew my ears were not deceiving me.

Tom had told us to remain silent through the sweat, but someone else was singing exactly an octave below Tom! It was as plain as day to me and stunning beyond belief. I craned around but could see no one else singing. We were instructed to remain in silence for the rest of the evening after the sweat but at breakfast I made a point of canvassing some of the other students.

"Did you hear anything funny in Tom's singing last night?"

Most didn't hear anything out of the ordinary. One said that one of the helpers outside was singing along, the idiot. Another said he thought he heard another voice.

Hours later, packed up and about to head for the airport, I brought it up to Tom.

"A few of us heard someone singing along with you last night during the sweat…"

"Um-hmm," Tom said.

"What was it?" I think he got pleasure from making me ask the obvious.

After a drag on his cigarette, Tom said casually, "Oh, that was Grandfather." He could just as well have said, "Oh, there comes the mailman."

"He always comes to the sweats. Sometimes he sings."

I nodded my complete understanding, thanked him, and walked away into a new world.

That new world led me up to this glorious moment, leaving the sweat lodge for the last time and exhilarating in laying my warm body on the cold ground and staring at the incredible night sky. Never had I felt more alive. With my body detached, my mind had soared to new realms inside the sweat lodge. I basked in the afterglow.

A shooting star left a glowing tail as it streaked from the zenith to the east. The east, I thought. Where the new day dawns, the direction of awakening and new beginnings.

# CHAPTER 23
# VISION QUEST

I STUCK MY HEAD out of the tiny tent and paid homage again to the east. Sunrise was a half hour away and Nick was walking toward my tent to awaken me. We nodded and smiled, each of us appreciating the synchronicity of the moment. He continued toward the next tent. I put things in order in my tent, stuffed my sleeping bag into its sack, and walked slowly to my spot.

What did I expect to get for sacrificing four days of activity and starving my body of food? Could I even do it? Would I go stir crazy or get too hungry? Would I get visions, signs, or symbols that would guide my life? What animals would I see and what might they mean to me?

Would my faith be built? Would I finally learn how to quiet my mind? Would I be visited by spirits I could see, hear, or feel?

I was an open book, ready for anything, but hoping -- at the very least -- to build a stronger bridge to the non-physical realm. My specific intentions had been written down months earlier, in one of several quest-preparation meetings with Scott. It had all led up to this early October morning.

I set my sleeping bag down with the water jugs on the east side of the tree and sat myself down on the west side. I watched the sun touch the treetops on the distant hill and work its way down into the little valley in front of me.

Whatever I expected, I didn't expect things to happen so soon. The sun wasn't on my shoulder yet so I know I hadn't been there an hour before I saw the coyote trotting up the valley to the west straight for me.

He had a jaunty gait as he climbed the hill on a path that would put him within a yard of my left shoulder if he continued straight. I watched his steady approach. When he was five yards from my circle he stopped. He seemed to me to be deciding which direction to take between two paths. His gaze never wavered; it was always toward the southeast though his body was facing east, toward me.

For five of the longest seconds of my life he stood there without moving. Then he headed south at the same gait and moved out of my view.

"Follow me," was the message I viscerally felt from the vacuum left in his absence.

I now had sensory overload and ninety-five more hours of quest in front of me. How was I going to think of anything else? Or quiet my mind? It was truly an amazing gift but it finally played out completely in my mind and I settled into the rhythm of the quest - the rhythm of sitting. And waiting. And doing nothing.

My mind went berserk on the second day. On the third day my body revolted. I barely had the strength to lift my water jugs. I noticed that I was only partially into the second gallon and, therefore, not drinking enough water. I pinched a tent of skin on the back of my hand. The ridge stayed up for a long time. I was badly dehydrated.

I began gulping water down. And peeing. And checking myself for dehydration. Why had I let myself get dehydrated? Was it the stern warning about recreational peeing? I found out later that the identical thing had happened to Alice. On day three she felt her quest was complete and walked out. With three and a quarter gallons of water remaining! She might as well have been on a water fast too.

Nick and Scott realized she was dehydrated and got her slugging down the fluids as she began the journaling process. It would take her another day to complete the journaling, and, in the complete silence of it, she continued the quest and had some of her most powerful experiences.

Although it may seem like four days sitting against a tree in the woods would be the four most boring days of your life, the opposite was true. Memories from those days are strong within me now, twelve years later.

Morning One was Morning of the Coyote, my most significant physical encounter. Afternoon One was the PM of the Chicken Business, a feeding frenzy for my starved mind. Night One was the Night of the Flying Squirrel who "flew" onto my tree just above me, my closest mammal encounter.

Morning Two was East Wind Morning, boding new beginnings and moisture. My mind stayed busy and my body was a wreck. I changed layers of clothes constantly to adjust my body temperature. Afternoon Two I slept restlessly. Night Two was Night of the Rain. I made a shelter of my ground cloth and stayed dry but cramped.

Morning Three brought West Wind and introspection. I was depleted and my back was sore. I finally realized I hadn't been drinking enough water so I slugged down huge amounts. Afternoon Three was the Beginning of the Dance. I had to move. I had been immobile for over 50 hours and my body rebelled. I had resisted the shuffling dance Scott had taught us, thinking it was a cop-out for weaklings. But it kept me in the game. I shuffled back and forth along an eight-foot line within my circle for minutes or hours, and then I'd collapse on the ground and have what I called "Little Visions."

Vivid movies ran through my head. In one I was yukking it up with my spirit guide, Mojo, a Native American who had a haircut like Moe of the Three Stooges. In another, Alice, a picture of naked beauty, leaned back and breathed fire. Others were visions of the past and future. I saw giant trees and natives rowing canoes. Then I saw the trees from above and they started waving like fields of grain. I realized they were under water. Then I saw a giant tree being cut and when it fell it was actually the statue of liberty!

There were many sensual and erotic visions, the most curious of which was a long series of different couples embraced in love but I could only see their heads – usually from a perspective of behind the woman. There were old, young, black, white. All were very blissful and in love.

Things became simpler during days three and four. I drank enough water, stopped changing clothes all the time by staying in underwear and sitting inside my sleeping bag when I was cold. The routine of dance and lie down worked well.

Afternoon Three featured Cloud Lessons as shapes morphed sometimes entertaining, sometimes teaching me. Finally a man blowing smoke at evening inspired me to take time for prayer. I began giving thanks and continued well into the dark.

Night Three was Night of the Stars and the Lynn Higbee dream. The skies had been cloudy the first two nights but were sparkling clear and clean after the rain of the second night. I watched Orion and the Pleiades and what looked like a coyote face in between them. Coyote teachings, yes! Some minutes later I noticed a semi-circle in between Orion and the coyote. Of course! His bow. Orion was the archer. Falling stars underscored revelations and pointed to significant directions for me.

I dreamt a vivid dream involving a good family friend who doted on his wife but wasn't true to himself. His wife called in distress from a plane. She was having trouble with oxygen and it sounded life threatening. I relayed the message that he needed to call her. He said, "No. I am going to get away." I tried to replay the message to him but couldn't get it to work. It had deep implications for my own relationship and me.

Day Four was Day of the Quail and Lusoto's Story. This last day of the quest was dominated by a vision of the last natives to live on this land, particularly a young man named Lusoto, and a story unfolded going back to the Spanish conquistadors. I dove deeply into this story and have spent a lot of time on it since.

A covey of quail came into my area. There must have been twenty. They shuffled and peeped along on the ground, coming within three feet of my circle. A few scouts hopped up into low branches of the cedar trees to search for danger.

And so my quest began with a lone coyote and finished with a covey of quail. That strikes me more clearly now as I reflect back on the "covey" of teachers, protectors, supporters, and friends I have found in my community of nature connection and awareness.

The most influential of those in my life have been three master trackers.

# Chapter 24
# Three Trackers

The thing about being influenced by master trackers is that you usually aren't aware you have been. Trained to make deductions on the slightest of cues, they are masters of the subtle, the nuance, the suggestion. They understand the power of giving "just enough information" to lead to "discovery for oneself." My personal experience with Tom Brown, Jon Young, and Allan Savory bears this out. My 'Aha!' moments seldom occurred during class or while reading their writings, but later, in thought or through experience.

The ultimate example of this is Tom Brown's mentoring of Jon Young for eight years in such a way that Jon never felt "taught." He felt inspired by Tom's mutual interest in his nature studies and curious by Tom's incessant questions but never for a moment – until one earth-shaking moment – considered that Tom might actually know some of the answers to the questions he was asking. And so profound was that realization to Jon that he has since devoted his life to mentoring youth and studying how knowledge is transferred in native cultures.

Although Allan Savory's teachings and writings are obviously gleaned from his considerable time on the land in Africa, few farmers, ranchers, business owners and governments using Holistic Management appreciate the important role tracking played in the development of Savory's resource management model. Quite simply, this model would not exist if Savory hadn't been a master tracker.

Nowhere is holistic thinking as ingrained as it is in the tracker who must be multi-tasking his senses and brain continuously. The eyes are the primary receiver of information – they follow the tracks. The eyes alternate between downward, focused on the track and sign to read its meaning; and upward, unfocused to pick up the slightest movements from the landscape within their full range of vision.

At the same time, the ears are always engaged - interpreting the bird language, the squirrel alarms, and all the sounds in the landscape. Often the only input a tracker receives is auditory. In one of Tom Brown's Standard classes a fox meandered along the field edge behind him. Tom appeared unaware until the fox had gone, and then he asked what the fox had done. Not only did he appear psychic for knowing the fox was there, he could relate much more about what the fox had done than his students could. In later classes we learned a little bird told him. Later still, we learned that Tom's tracker mind could stay focused on teaching while decoding the birdcalls in the background.

Even the lack of sound is vital information to the tracker. It means something when the crickets and frogs go quiet, when certain birds stop calling. The concept of listening for anomalies and quiet zones within a 360-degree "sound-scape" boggles the mind of the non-tracker. We are not accustomed to listening for silence or for distant sounds.

One moist morning when the sound was traveling exceptionally well, I listened to the neighbor boy's entire drive to work in his souped-up truck. It was a fifteen-mile trip.

The tactile senses are heightened on a trail, particularly through the feet. To the native, the feet have eyes of their own and there is no need to look down to place them carefully. Tracking is done barefoot or in thin moccasins so the feet sense the ground, taking in information, giving back as little as possible in their silent, careful placements. The skin and hairs on the cheeks and forearms feel the wind direction and humidity, both of which are used by trackers.

The sense of smell reaches out and collects data continuously. Many animals have distinctive scent trails detectable by the trained human nose. Trees and plants put out olfactory information that can be useful. Even water can be smelled by the master tracker. Tom Brown's teacher, an elder Apache, could, by smell alone, distinguish between the water flowing in several creeks where he lived.

When all these senses are engaged simultaneously, a synergistic magic happens. Other senses come into play for which we have no names, nor formal teaching. They are collectively the "gut" sense, the intuitive hit. Some interpret it as smell or a physical sensation but the knowing comes to us from beyond our five physical senses. In the master tracker, therefore, not only is his logical, deductive mind continually exercised in sleuthing a trail, but his intuitive sense also becomes razor sharp.

In native cultures, the best trackers provide the most food, become the best scouts, and eventually take on leadership roles. Do smart people choose to track or does tracking make people smarter? Perhaps both, but there is no doubt that the tracker brain is developed in ways that can't be replicated otherwise. From the constant exercise of pushing the physical senses to their limits and beyond, trackers experience a state of heightened awareness unavailable to most.

So powerful are the faculties gained in tracking and so influential have these three trackers been in my own development that this writing felt incomplete without acknowledging them and underscoring their significance.

## Allan Savory

The word "tracker" as a description of Allan Savory rightfully follows other words: ecologist, visionary, statesman, soldier, author, and educator. Nonetheless, Allan is very much a tracker and was my first tracker-mentor.

He gave a speech in Des Moines in the 1980s that had an enormous impact on me. In it, he fully lived up to his reputation as a cantankerous white African. His speech was meticulously organized and methodical and followed this logic: The best agricultural practices had destroyed land, wiped out populations, and created deserts while animals running free maintained lush, healthy ecosystems that built soil. What was the difference?

Like Darwin studying the curiosities of the Galapagos, it took him decades, punctuated by four key insights, to satisfactorily explain why the human system failed and nature's worked. Since then he has refined a model of holistic decision-making that insures resource enhancement. Now his life is devoted to teaching others how to implement it.

To further appreciate the tracker's mind, it pays to note his four key insights: The first is that nature functions on a systems level where everything interacts; nothing is isolated. Every organism participates in a larger system interacting with other organisms in complex ways. The word he found to describe this key insight was holism, coined by fellow white African statesman and soldier, Jan Smuts.

The second key insight helped him understand why he saw land degrading rapidly in Africa but not in England. This he called environmental brittleness, an indicator of the fragility of the soils. More specifically, it deals with how organic matter is broken down in humid versus arid environments, a phenomenon previously unnoticed. Since the important process of organic-matter decomposition differs radically in varying humidities, proper management must account for those differences. Thus, Savory devised a "brittleness" scale from one to ten, one being desert, ten being rainforest.

The next key insight, of great appeal to farmers and ranchers, is that animal herd effect heals the land. We only need consider the wildebeest of the Serengeti, the caribou of the Arctic, and the bison of the Great Plains. Their massive impact - through bunching to avoid predators and migration to avoid dung and urine and find fresh grass– molded the vast grazing lands of the earth. The hooves tilled and planted, the teeth and tongue pruned, the digestive system fertilized. The herd effect shaped the evolution of diverse prairie communities. Savory contends that the herd effect is, practically speaking, the only way to heal land.

The last key insight demystified the damaging effects of overgrazing by clarifying how small numbers of cattle do it while massive herds of wild animals do not. Overgrazing is not a function of numbers of animals on an area, but a function of time the animals are on an area. After grazing, a plant's carbohydrate root reserves are called up to make new leaves, new photosynthetic material. If that regrowth occurs and another graze happens before photosynthesis replaces the underground reserves, the plant suffers a net energy loss. Since man has been in charge there has been a continuous depletion of soil energy the world over.

I liken it to the game of musical chairs where, one by one, the players are eliminated when the music stops and one chair-less person leaves the game. In an un-rested pasture, plant species are eliminated one by one as their root reserves are depleted by overgrazing of the succulent regrowth. Finally, all that remains is the species most adapted to this game – the one with the least succulent regrowth.

The "winning features" of the last standing species are simply one: Early maturity. The plant that gets fibrous first will be the least re-bitten. Looked at from the other side, the plants that stay succulent longer will be the most re-bitten. Consequently, pastures the world over have, when livestock over-grazed them, diminished from diverse prairies with species maturing all season long to monocultures of the local, early-maturing species. The fields have a nice early spring growth but are relatively inactive for the rest of the "growing" season. The loss of land productivity is phenomenal.

Form inexorably following function, a diverse prairie polyculture reduces to monoculture simply with traditional, "musical chairs" grazing. The good news, however, is startling: The reverse is also true!

Mimicking the bunched graze-and-migrate behavior of large, wild herds allows optimal photosynthetic energy accumulation and stimulates diversification from monoculture toward prairie. Indeed, it is the only way to create prairie! Merely planting seeds is a waste of time if the prairie-inducing "function" of herd effect is not applied. Using Savory's four key insights, land managers around the globe are bringing back prairies, increasing soil organic matter, and, the ultimate proof, raising water tables.

The effect of hearing Savory expound upon these Darwinian observations and deductions is staggering. What emerges is a new worldview and understanding of the interplay of agriculture and ecology and the rise and fall of civilizations. Followed quickly by a keen desire to implement nature-mimicking, soil-building, grazing techniques.

As a consequence of this understanding, I have devoted much of my life to inspiring others – both livestock producers and red meat consumers – to support properly managed, grassfed livestock. This endeavor has come a long way in twenty-five years and has gained steam - especially with Michael Pollan's brilliant writing and Joel Salatin's eloquent example. With the pen and the sword of these brilliant men leading the way, responsible land stewardship and exceptional meat products gain popularity daily.

The extent to which Allan's tracking mastery affected his life work came home to me only after knowing him for twenty years and developing my own appreciation of the art and science of tracking. I learned that Allan obsessed over the bush in his boyhood Rhodesia. He taught himself to track, pushing himself to the point of coming to the end of a lion trail – that is, flushing the lion – after hired-gun professionals had quit the trail because of the danger of darkness and thickening vegetation. Allan tracked the rogue cattle killer on hands and knees, "feel tracking" in the dark under the leaves, not to destroy the lion but to prove that a teenager who could master fear could 'out-track' fearful professionals.

He defied age barriers, entering prematurely both the Rhodesian game service and, later, the military. As an under-aged private he walked to the front lines where communist-backed Zambian and Mozambique troops were terrorizing Rhodesians. There, he reported in as "Sergeant Savory." Discovering - and admiring - his bluff later, they allowed him to retain his self-designated rank. He then convinced his superiors to allow him to train troops in tactical tracking and irregular warfare – skills he had honed hunting down heavily armed elephant and rhino poachers.

The Tracker Combat Unit, which was formed under Savory's command and training, deftly did its job with insurgents. The organization became the model for military and police tracking units worldwide. One of its early students, David Scott-Donelan, founded the preeminent Tactical Tracking Operations School in the United States. Many military, police and corrections personnel who are trained in tracking – just like many of us who apply holistic management - are unaware of the debt of gratitude we owe for our mentor's (or mentor's mentor's) dirt time tracking in the bush of Africa.

## Tom Brown Jr.

Tom Brown Jr. is nothing more than a storyteller who makes up people and events to serve his own interests. Or Tom Brown Jr. is one of the most skilled people alive today. You choose.

Also known as "The Tracker," Tom Brown has a traceable track record of hunting down fugitives, finding hundreds of lost people, some of them still alive, and training Navy Seals and other special forces. That much is known.

With Tom I had to shed much of who I was and start over. Literally, I relearned to sit, stand, walk, and run. I had been doing them all wrong. At my first class, the famous "Standard," my back was so uncomfortable sitting all day that I was constantly fidgeting and trying to get relief. Now I can easily sit still as a stone for an hour with insects landing and crawling on me. (This may not be your life's aspiration, but to a native, it's a basic survival skill.)

When I started the Standard class I walked and ran on my toes, my heels barely touching the ground. It was as if I wasn't of the earth, I was of the air. Bringing my body down, slowing it, and grounding it has changed who I am and how I interact with the world.

These fundamental changes are the beginning of a huge set of skills taught in Tom's many classes, most of which Alice and I took. But as much as I enjoyed learning survival, tracking, and awareness skills from Tom, what fascinates me most is the unknown and unverifiable world that Tom describes where tracking, survival, and awareness skills are the springboard to unimaginable experiences in the non-physical realm.

Unimaginable experiences like hearing Grandfather Stalking Wolf sing in the sweat lodge, hearing drumming on prayer hill, and having crystalline visions on scores of guided meditations.

Like Savory, Tom has a skill set that goes far beyond tracking, but the tracking is what develops the mind, fine-tunes the reasoning faculties, and pushes the senses beyond the physical realm. In my own limited way, I had to test those skills of his for myself. Partly I was playing with the teacher; partly I was proving to myself that he was who he implied he was.

One of my early tests was to stand on the far side of a tree along a road I knew he would soon travel. I just stood there close to the tree facing the road in my dull woods clothes. As his four-wheeler whizzed past, Tom's head did a quick 90-degree swivel to look right at me. The head instructor of the camp, seated on the back of the four-wheeler and facing me, never saw me.

At another class, I sometimes snuck into the instructor's facilities in the early morning hours to take a delicious hot shower, otherwise unavailable to the hundred-odd students. One morning I snuck into the bathroom used by Tom and left a virtually indiscernible trail that led to the ceiling.

That morning Tom came straight in to the lecture hall after driving from his home and said, "The weirdest thing happened to me this morning. When I walked in to the bathroom there was a nose hair stuck on the ceiling. Now how could that nose hair have gotten on the ceiling?" To my utter amazement he kept up the banter about the nose hair on the ceiling for several minutes.

When you play mind games with Tom you soon realize you aren't in the same league. Too many times to doubt, I've seen Tom refer to things that happened out on an exercise that he didn't physically witness. Tom's awareness seemed to go everywhere, but you were never sure.

He tells countless stories of Grandfather's skills of awareness. My favorite story of distant vision takes place in a weekend camp with Grandfather. Rick, Tom's woods partner and grandson of Grandfather, had set up traps with Tom on their way to camp. When the boys arrived, they were told by Grandfather that it would be a fasting camp.

They made camp and sat silently around a small fire as the night deepened, Grandfather appearing asleep although he never was. Then Grandfather's head popped up and he said, "Tom, your deadfall missed him." The boys wondered in silence, "Missed who? How did he know Tom had made a deadfall trap?"

A few minutes later, Grandfather's head popped up again and he said, "Rick, your snare got the rabbit."

That was all the boys could take. At the first chance they ran back in the luminescent light of the Pine Barrens night to the distant site of the traps. By this point the boys were already good trackers and could piece together that, indeed, the same rabbit that tripped Tom's deadfall was caught a few minutes later by Rick's snare.

They ran back to camp with the rabbit and breathlessly asked Grandfather (who was always awake, remember) how he knew what had happened. He answered with surprise, "Wouldn't you know it if a creature was walking on your back?"

Hundreds of similar stories inspired us students to adopt a mindset open to all possibilities, a native mindset free of the limits of modernity. And from that mind opening followed our own otherworldly experiences of feeling things moving on the landscape, tracking an animal's spirit, communicating to each other without words, and other formerly impossible things.

A mind opened in such a way has an awareness level far beyond normal. To it the landscape sings a continuous song.

With Jon Young I experienced that song through the eyes and ears of the most aware community left on earth, the Kalahari Bushmen.

## Jon Young

Like many of Tom's students I had never heard of Jon Young. He had no reputation preceding him, no books written yet, no gunshot wounds, no gigantic aura like Tom. In fact, I didn't even notice him hanging around our Advanced Awareness class.

Then Tom orchestrated one of the best pieces of teaching I've ever seen. He called our twelve groups of eight people each to get within our groups and walk to the Iroquois campground where there were some interesting claw tracks on a pole he wanted to show us. We walked the hundred yards to the camp area and, when all were assembled, Tom looked at his watch and said, "Oh. Brain fart! It's too close to lunch to do this exercise. Let's break for lunch and meet back at the lecture hall at 1:00."

At one o'clock Tom said, "Get in your groups and draw a map of the walk to the Iroquois camp. Note everything on it. Go!"

Oh boy, this is what we loved! We were on it like a hen on a June bug. Drawing trails and plants and trees and noting where the sun was and the wind direction, this is what we were – trackers with super awareness.

He wrapped us up in half an hour and called for a representative of group five to bring up their map and report. It was an awesome exhibit with a great map and, huh, even some stuff our group didn't get, but we had more. When the group-five representative had exhausted their report, Tom called upon a group-nine representative to come up and list anything group five hadn't. A much shorter version followed and still our group had some extras, but fewer.

After the next two groups were called and gave very short reports, Tom asked if any group still had more to add. A few answers were called out. Tom let the silence incubate.

"Jon, what did you see?"

A thin, unassuming guy with a downward-looking, shy appearance walked to the front where the presenters had been. Time warped at that point for me because what followed rocked my world. I was transported to a Rudyard Kipling story about Kim, a young Indian boy trained to record everything in his mind after just one glance.

Jon closed his eyes and began talking softly, almost poetically. He spoke of the animals that had traveled down or across our path the night before. He talked about what had happened in the early morning. It was as if he were in a trance and transported back to witness it all. When he finally got to our actual walk he described how far the junco alarms had carried from our group and how the birds had hooked up into the nearby whatever trees to watch us while they waited us out.

For twenty minutes he went on with beautiful words and flowing language of what had happened, all in chronological order. The detail was endless. It seemed as if he could speak on it for the rest of his life.

Tom finally said softly, "Thank you, Jon. That's enough."

Who was this guy?

Jon and Tom met long ago, about the time Grandfather left the picture. Grandfather had mentored Tom for about ten years, from the age of eight to eighteen.

When they met, Jon was ten, eight years Tom's junior. For the next eight years, Jon was Tom's student, but only Tom knew it. Jon thought Tom was just an older friend who had a really cool skull collection and liked to camp out in the woods but really didn't know very much. And was actually kind of slow in the head about a lot of stuff.

For the entire eight-year apprenticeship, Tom played dumb with Jon. His teaching method was simply to pique Jon's curiosity. He asked Jon endless questions about what he had been seeing in the woods lately.

They developed a routine that went like this. After dinner Tom would call up.

"Hi Jon."

"Hi Tom."

"Whatcha do today?"

"Oh I was down in the river fishin' and swimmin' and messin' around."

"Oh yeah? Were the fish biting?"

"I caught a couple of nice bluegills."

"Um-hmm. What was going on down there?"

"Oh not much. But a couple of little brown birds showed up after I laid down a while."

"Did you get a good look at them?"

"I tried but they stayed just out of site in the bushes. "

"Oh….You suppose they have a nest down there or something?"

"Yeah…maybe!"

And then Jon would be thinking about where the bird nest was, and that he could identify the secretive birds by their eggs and nest and he couldn't wait to go back and explore.

Tom always took a subject that Jon had a lot of interest in – birds, for example – and he'd find the edge of Jon's awareness, leaving Jon re-creating in his own mind the possible answers and determined to check back to find them out.

It didn't take too many conversations like this before Jon knew that his inquisitive friend (who was too lazy to learn all this stuff on his own!) would probably ask him in detail about what he had seen, so he continually looked harder and deeper, observed more. The constant rewards his curiosity brought him piqued his curiosity ever more.

He gradually developed that recall-at-a-glance ability. As his knowledge of the woods deepened, he learned patterns such as how Juncos react to a large group of people and what typically happens on a trail at night in the Pine Barrens of New Jersey in any given season. In tracking and nature awareness Jon became at an early age the equivalent of a grandmaster in chess.

Reading a trail with me in the spectacular early morning of the Great Kalahari desert in Botswana, he was a child again. A child on Christmas morning. There was so much that had happened during the night! A typical night in the Kalahari made tracking anywhere in America dull by comparison.

The canines alone were fascinating. Look at the huge front track of a brown hyena! He probably weighs a hundred pounds! He gets as big as our largest canine, the gray wolf. But he doesn't get nearly as big as his cousin, the spotted hyena, which can reach 185 pounds! In packs, those guys dominate lions.

Look at these delicate tracks of two, nearly equal-sized, small canines. Can you see the differences? Jon's eyes briefly leave the tracks to twinkle the question. Uncharacteristically, in his Christmas excitement, Jon downloads recently memorized facts. These tracks are probably from the bat-eared fox and the jackal.

Jon repeated aloud shoulder height and stride details from the field guides, inviting us to look at the tiny hair tracks between the toes as we followed one set. Then he burst out laughing, "Look at that crazy dung beetle track!"

This incredible trip occurred twelve years after being blown away by Jon's recall in the Tracker class, five years after my yearlong apprenticeship with Jon. Called the "Protégé Program," Jon took a small group under wing for a year to replicate with us the manner in which he was taught by Tom Brown Jr. It was one of the great privileges of my life.

There was no instruction in the traditional K through 12 and college sense. We were mentored like children, allowing our interests and capacities for digestion to dictate our activities and our weekly assignments. What emerges in this process is an organic, holistic learning process where one interest leads down a trail that has many side trails, each of which might have side trails of its own and on and on until all trails overlap and interconnect to create a large tapestry that is one's home area, complete with seasonal colors and textures and patterns.

I came away not with facts so much as a more complete understanding of the wildlife interactions around my farm and a deep appreciation of the interconnectedness of everything. As a long-time land manager, I realized more than ever the importance of Allan Savory's first insight in Holistic management – that everything is interconnected and every decision we land owners make ripples deeply through the ecosystem.

Native minds never know any other than an interconnected world. But you and I weren't raised that way, unless you were more fortunate than I. We have the modern reductionist mind that considers as few variables as possible in a problem to isolate "the" one solution. Separation - rather than community - thinking.

The world is waking up to the realization that reductionist thinking can never solve environmental problems; it only creates new ones. Looking for the single best action to "save the earth," like clean up the oceans or sequester carbon or get off oil is still reductionist thinking.

Until we have a critical mass of people thinking holistically, the decision-making process will remain flawed. The simple answer is to raise tracker children. When we put kids in nature with a track to follow, the mind blossoms organically in all directions. The attention is taken in many directions at once; the mind fully engages. After a few years of tapestry weaving, the holistic nature of nature is embedded and it becomes impossible to make decisions in isolation.

The human mind evolved to do this. Kalahari Bushmen epitomize the complete human. Their eyes and smiles tell it all. They miss nothing, accept everything, and exist in harmony with their world. The children are masters at mimicking games, focusing, and getting along with others.

Interacting with these three master trackers rocked my world. They took me back to ground zero and taught me how to crawl again, how to walk again, how to run again, how to sit again, how to see and hear again, how to heal land and, for the first time, how to be really still and how to fully experience nature and myself.

# CHAPTER 25
# FINDING MYSELF

FULLY EXPERIENCING MYSELF means aligning my thoughts, beliefs, speech, attitudes and actions - the outward expression of me - with the inner essence, the spirit, of me. My inner essence is focused, all-knowing, unwavering, and eternal. The outward expression of me, this clump of flesh called David, plays a continuous, clumsy game of pin-the-tail-on-the-donkey of happiness. 'You're getting hot,' 'You're getting cold,' my emotions tell me as I stumble around, poking blindly.

With my quieter, more attentive self, I listen to what my emotions are telling me and move, more and more, toward the feelings of happiness. It is not rocket science to know what makes me happy. But it is amazing how I have trained myself to ignore my feelings. Or, more accurately, *untrained* myself since I was born with a perfectly accurate guidance system.

When I am happy it is because the outer me has lined up with the inner me and I'm doing or thinking something that is true to who I am, pinning the tail right on the donkey's rear end. When I am unhappy it is because whatever I am doing or thinking is not true to who I am. In nature's perfect feedback loop, my emotions express exactly how connected I am to my true self. Bliss = right on; depression = not even close.

Everything is vibration and seeking happiness may be defined as a simple exercise in discerning if I am in harmony with my own vibrations. Harmony feels good; dissonance feels bad. Hot. Cold. Knowing that my emotions express how nearly I am aligned outwardly and inwardly has been a complete game changer in my life.

Here's the logic sequence:

I believe there is a broader, non-physical me.

I believe I am aligned when my outward me and inward me are on the same wavelength.

I believe I can tell my nearness to my broader me by how good I feel.

I want to be in alignment with the broader me as much as possible.

Therefore, my goal is simply to follow my bliss.

How close do you want to be with your God, your inner being, your source, Nature, or whatever term you may use to define the almighty and unknown 'man behind the curtain' of your life? Or, if you believe there is no man, how happy do you want to be? Very happy? Then try out this formula.

When I realized the answer to my spiritual connection and happiness was totally in my hands, that I made my choices thousands of times daily with my decisions, it caused a complete reorganization of my thought process. If my thoughts are the seeds of everything in my life and I do reap what I sow, that is where I must post my 'thought editor,' my sentinel, my bouncer, my weed hoer. When a negative thought sprouts, my bouncer hopefully catches it in his negative thought net and keeps it from exiting my mouth in words until I find a silver lining to it. Then I lovingly release it.

For example, let's say the following ticker tape runs through my mind on a rushed drive, "What is this moron doing driving 45 on a 60 mph road?" Bouncer is activated before another condemning thought follows and I become pensive. I observe it is an elderly lady. A lot like my grandma who wouldn't give up driving. Well, good for her. I bet she doesn't get out very much. I'm not in that big a hurry. My, the fall colors are really starting to show! It does me good to slow down sometime and appreciate what's around me.

"Aren't the colors gorgeous right now?" are the words that leave my mouth.

I am this vigilant and devoted to the positive spin because I understand that the positive or negative nature of my thoughts going out determines the positive or negative nature of my life experience coming back. My outward signal is also my inward signal in any moment. If I broadcast on KPU I can only receive on KPU. If I broadcast on AOK I can only receive on AOK. It is as if there is only one highway in and out of David on any subject and at any moment of any day I get to choose which is open, the Bliss Highway or the Down in the Dumps Highway or any highway between.

I can't get bliss when I'm in the dumps. And I can't get dumped on when I'm in bliss. It's a law of physical particle attraction that includes the attractive nature of our thoughts. You can try this for yourself but I warn you, if you do you will be confronted with some very difficult decisions.

The human experience is more often than not one of putting up with a lot, sacrificing our happiness for a less-than-perfect job because it pays the bills, or enduring a body condition we don't feel good about, or interacting with a mate in disempowering ways. If and when you put the negative thought editor in place, there are no excuses for negative thoughts anymore.

"Because it pays the bills," is bogus; I am holding myself back from a more empowered job.

"It is a genetic condition," is a lame excuse to remain in a compromised health condition.

And - my big one - "So many other things about the relationship are fabulous," is a disempowering cop out.

I realized I was riding the So-so Highway on the subject of relationship. As much good as there was, there were also deeply ingrained, disempowering aspects that were too big for me to 'silver-line' away. We both arrived there, both knew, and both knew that the silver lining would come in the form of more empowering future relationships with others. With our greater clarity about what the relationship donkey looks like we can more accurately pin its tail and travel on the Bliss Highway frequency.

To us, our separation is a testimony to our belief in the power of attentiveness to our happiness. As difficult as it was to separate, we knew we were releasing the other, and ourselves, toward better, toward more. In that sense, separation is an act of monumental courage and honor and love for the other and self. That it is often seen by family and community as failure makes the act even more fearless.

Ralph Waldo Emerson, in his essay on self reliance, said, "To be great is to be misunderstood." Letting go of what others may think is critical to our search for ourselves. Only the lead dog gets to watch the scenery change and we are both enjoying the new view of relationship.

With my life expanding in new and exciting ways and my thoughts more on the Bliss Highways, the world has opened to me more than ever before, creating more ways to empower others, and seeing more of the world as I do it. But always I come back to community values, my beloved quiet time in nature, and being thankful for my simple country existence. More and more I am finding myself in the country.

CPSIA information can be obtained at www.ICGtesting.com
Printed in the USA
LVOW062128301112

309491LV00002B/7/P